S0-ACC-429

THE EUROPEAN WORLD, 400–1450

BONNIE G. SMITH

GENERAL EDITOR

THE EUROPEAN WORLD, 400–1450

Barbara A. Hanawalt

To my mentors, Margaret Hasting and Peter Charanis,
who taught me to enjoy the story in history.

OXFORD
UNIVERSITY PRESS

Oxford University Press, Inc., publishes works that further
Oxford University's objective of excellence
in research, scholarship, and education.

Oxford New York
Auckland Cape Town Dar es Salaam Hong Kong Karachi
Kuala Lumpur Madrid Melbourne Mexico City Nairobi
New Delhi Shanghai Taipei Toronto

With offices in
Argentina Austria Brazil Chile Czech Republic France Greece
Guatemala Hungary Italy Japan Poland Portugal Singapore
South Korea Switzerland Thailand Turkey Ukraine Vietnam

Published by Oxford University Press, Inc.
198 Madison Avenue, New York, New York 10016
www.oup.com

Oxford is a registered trademark of Oxford University Press

Design: Stephanie Blumenthal and Alexis Siroc
Cover design and logo: Nora Wertz

Library of Congress Cataloging-in-Publication Data

Hanawalt, Barbara.
The European world, 400–1450 / Barbara A. Hanawalt.
p. cm. — (The medieval and early modern world)
Includes bibliographical references and index.
ISBN-13: 978-019-517844-9 — ISBN-13: 978-019-522267-8 (Calif. ed.) — ISBN-13: 978-019-522157-2 (set)
ISBN-10: 0-19-517844-0 — ISBN-10: 0-19-522267-9 (Calif. ed.) — ISBN-10: 0-19-522157-5 (set)
1. Middle Ages—History. 2. Civilization, Medieval. 3. Europe—History—476-1492. I. Title. II. Series.
D117.H25 2005
940.1—dc22
2004019146

9 8 7 6 5 4 3 2 1

Printed in the United States on acid-free paper.

On the cover: An ivory chess piece from 12th-century France is carved with a tournament scene.
Frontispiece: A 14th-century king of France makes a royal entry into a city with his queen.

BONNIE G. SMITH
GENERAL EDITOR

DIANE L. BROOKS, ED.D.
EDUCATION CONSULTANT

The European World, 400–1450
Barbara A. Hanawalt

The African and Middle Eastern World, 600–1500
Randall Pouwels

The Asian World, 600–1500
Roger Des Forges and John S. Major

An Age of Empires, 1200–1750
Marjorie Wall Bingham

An Age of Voyages, 1350–1600
Merry E. Wiesner-Hanks

An Age of Science and Revolutions, 1600–1800
Toby E. Huff

The Medieval and Early Modern World: Primary Sources & Reference Volume
Donald R. Kelley and Bonnie G. Smith

CONTENTS

A ❝ marks a primary source—a piece of writing that speaks to us from the past.

MARE NAVIGAVIT ET VE

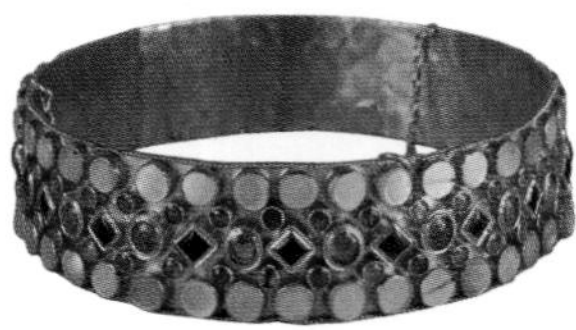

CAST OF CHARACTERS

Abelard (AB-uh-lard), Peter 1079–1142 • French scholar and teacher

Albigensians (AL-buh-JEN-shuns) • 13th-century heretical Christian group that believed there was a good and an evil God, also known as Cathars

Alfred, 849–901 • King of Wessex (871–901); saved England from Viking invaders in the 870s

Ambrose (AM-broze), 340–397 • Bishop of Milan who preached to Augustine

Anglo-Saxons • Germanic peoples who settled in England in the fifth century

Apollinaris (uh-PALL-uh-NAR-us), Sidonius (sigh-DOE-nee-us), 431–489 • Roman bishop who married the emperor's daughter; organized the city's defense against the Visigoths in the 470s

Aquinas (uh-KWAI-nus), Thomas, 1225–1274 • Scholar and Dominican friar; wrote *Summa Theologica*

Arians (AIR-ee-uns) • Followers of the Roman monk Arius who believed that Jesus was human, not divine

Athaulf (AT-haulf), died 1415 • Visigoth king who led his people into Spain

Attila the Hun (uh-TIL-uh), 406–453 • Leader of the Huns from 433 to 453; tried to invade the western Roman Empire

Augustine (aw-GUS-teen), 354–430 • Roman nobleman who converted to Christianity

à Becket (a-BEK-ut), **Thomas** (TOM-us), 1118–1170 • Archbishop of Canterbury; exiled by Henry II and then martyred

Bede (BEED), 673–735 • Benedictine monk known as the Venerable Bede; wrote *The Ecclesiastical History of the English People*

Benedict (BEN-uh-dikt), 480–547 • Founder of the Benedictine order of monks and author of the Benedictine Rule

Boccaccio (bo-KOCH-chee-oh), **Giovanni** (jee-oh-VAN-ee), 1313–1375 • Italian poet who wrote *The Decameron* during the plague

Bohemund (BO-uh-mund), 1057–1111 • Leader of the First Crusade who founded the Principality of Antioch

Boniface VIII (BON-uh-fus), 1235–1303 • Pope named in 1294 after Celestine V resigned; quarreled with Philip IV of France

Capet (ka-PAY), Hugh, 938–996 • King of France starting in 987; began the Capetian dynasty

Celestine V (SEL-uh-steen), 1210–1296 • Pope who resigned in 1294 because of papal corruption

Charlemagne (SHAR-luh-mane), 742–814 • Founder of the Carolingian dynasty in France; expanded the territory of the Franks

Charles VII, 1403–1461 • Prince of France who was encouraged by Joan of Arc to pursue his claim to the throne

Clotilda (kluh-TIL-duh), about 475–545 • Queen of the Franks; converted her husband, Clovis, to Christianity

Clovis (KLOW-vus), 465–511 • King who unified the Franks and started the Merovingian dynasty

Comnenus (kom-NEE-nus), **Alexius** (uh-LEK-see-us), 1048–1118 • Byzantine emperor whose appeal to Pope Urban II in 1094 led to the First Crusade

Constantine the Great (KON-stun-teen), about 285–337 • First Roman emperor to convert to Christianity

Datini (dah-TEE-nee), Francesco de Marco (fran-CHE-sko-de-MAR-kow), 1335–1410 • Merchant who lived in Italy and France and survived the plague

Díaz (DEE-as), **Rodrigo** (rod-REE-go), 1043–1099 • Nobleman who fought in the *Reconquista*;inspired the poem *El Cid*

Dominic (DOM-uh-nik), 1170–1221 • Founder of the Order of Friar Preachers, or Dominicans

Dominicans (dow-MIN-uh-kuns) • Brotherhood of monks who lived among the poor, preached, and taught at universities

Edward, 1003–1066 • King of England called the Confessor because of his pious habits

Edward I, 1239–1307 • King of England who came to the throne in 1272; legal reformer

Eleanor of Aquitaine (ah-KWI-tane), 1122–1204 • Ruler of France and England at different times whose court was a center of art and culture

Ferdinand (FUR-di-nand), 1452–1516 • King of Aragon; started the Inquisition with his wife, Queen Isabella

Francis of Assisi (uh-SEE-zee), 1182–1226 • Merchant who underwent a religious conversion and founded the Franciscan order of monks

Franks • Germanic people who invaded and settled France

Frederick I Barbarossa (BAR-buh-row-suh), 1123–1190 • Emperor of Germany who drowned on his way to the Third Crusade

Frederick II, 1194–1250 • Grandson of Frederick I Barbarossa; ruled Germany starting in 1212

Galla Placidia (pluh-SID-ee-uh), Galla, 388–450 • Sister of a Roman emperor who married the Visigoth king Athaulf

Gerbert of Aurillac (AW-ri-lak), died 1003 • Peasant who was made Pope Sylvester II by the German emperor in 999

Godwinson (GOD-win-sun), Harold (Harold II), 1022–1066 Brother of King Edward's wife, Edith; tried to claim the English throne in 1066

Gregory of Tours (tour), 539–594 • Bishop of Tours who wrote a history of the Franks

Guiscard (GEES-kar), **Robert,** 1015–1085 • Norman ruler who conquered southern Italy

Gutenberg (GOO-tun-burg), **Johann** (yo-HON), 1397–1468 • Inventor of the movable-type printing press; printed the first German-language Bible in 1455

Hardrada (HARD-ra-duh), **Harald** (HAR-uld), 1015–1066 • King of Norway who tried to claim the English throne in 1066

Héloïse (EL-oh-weez), 1101–1164 • Abbess of the Oratory of the Paraclete

Henry II, 1133–1189 • King of England who married Eleanor of Aquitaine; started legal reforms in England

Henry III, 1207–1272 • Son of King John I; became King of England in 1216 when he was nine years old

Hildebrand (HIL-duh-brant), 1023–1085 • Cluniac monk who developed the College of Cardinals; named Pope Gregory VII in 1073

Huns • Nomadic people from central Asia who attacked the Roman Empire

Hus (HOOS), **Jan** (yaun), 1370–1415 • He started a religious movement based on Wycliffe's ideas; he was burned as a heretic

Ibn Khaldun (ib-UN-kal-DOON), 1332–1395 • Arab historian who held various offices under the rulers of Tunis and Morocco

Innocent III (IN-uh-sent), 1161–1216 • Guardian of German emperor Frederick II; became pope in 1198

Isabella (iz-uh-BEL-uh), 1451–1504 • Queen of Castile; united Spain with her husband, King Ferdinand of Aragon

Joan of Arc (ARK), 1412–1431 • French woman who fought in the Hundred Years War; believed that she heard the voices of saints

John I, 1167–1216 • King of England after his brother Richard's death; called John Lackland

Justinian (juh-STIN-ee-un), 483–565 • Byzantine emperor from 527 to 565; made a unified code of law and rebuilt Constantinople

Langton (LANG-tun), Stephen, 1150–1228 • English archbishop who led revolt that resulted in the Magna Carta

Lombards (lum-BARDS) • Germanic tribe that settled in northern Italy

Louis I (LOO-ee), 778–840 • Son of Charlemagne who ruled after his death

Louis VII, 1120–1180 • King of France, starting in 1137; had his marriage to Eleanor of Aquitaine annulled

Martel, Charles, 688–741 • King of the Franks called the Hammer of Christendom for turning back Islamic invaders in 732

Merovingians (mer-uh-VIN-juns) • Frankish dynasty founded by Clovis

Moors (mors) • European name for the Muslims who occupied the Iberian Peninsula starting in the eighth century

Muhammad (mo-HA-mud), 571–632 • Prophet who founded the religion of Islam

Normans • Vikings who settled the Atlantic coast of France whose descendants conquered England in 1066

Otto I the Great, 912–973 • King of Germany; took the title of Roman emperor in 962

Patrick, Saint, around 389–461 • Missionary who converted the Irish to Christianity

Pépin (PEP-un), 714–768 • Father of Charlemagne; had himself declared king of France in 751

Persians (PUR-zhuns) • Muslims who inhabited modern-day Iran

Peter of Aragon, 1239–1285 • Spainish king; took Sicily in 1282

Peter, Saint, died 64 • One of Jesus' original followers; said to have founded the Church of Rome

Philip II Augustus (aw-GUS-tus), 1165–1223 • King of France who fought with English kings over Angevin territory; took Normandy from John I

Philip IV (FIL-up), 1268–1314 • King of France who fought with Edward I of England; expelled the Jews in 1306

Plantagenet (plan-TAJ-uh-nit), **Geoffrey** (jef-REE), 1110–1151 • Count of Anjou who conquered Normandy in 1144; his son became Henry II

Procopius (pruh-KO-pee-us), 6th century • Court historian of Byzantine emperor Justinian

Richard II, 1367–1400 • King of England; came to throne in 1377 when he was 10; was king during the Revolt of 1381

Richard the Lion-Hearted, 1157–1199 • Son of Henry II and Eleanor of Aquitaine; crowned king of England in 1189

Roswitha (ros-VEET-uh) of **Gandersheim** (gan-DER-shime), 935–972 • Benedictine nun and German scholar who wrote poetry, plays, and histories

Scholastica (sko-LAS-tik-uh), 480–543 • Sister of Benedict; patron saint of Benedictine nuns

Seljuk Turks • Nomadic central Asian tribes people who converted to Islam and conquered the Near East in the 11th century

Tancred (TANG-krud), 1072–1112 • Nephew of Behemond who also participated in the First Crusade; later served as regent of Antioch

Theodora (theo-DOOR-uh), 500–548 • Ruled the Byzantines with her husband, Justinian

Urban II, 1042–1099 • Pope who preached a sermon in 1095 that called for the First Crusade

Vikings • Scandinavian warriors who raided throughout Europe in the 9th and 10th centuries

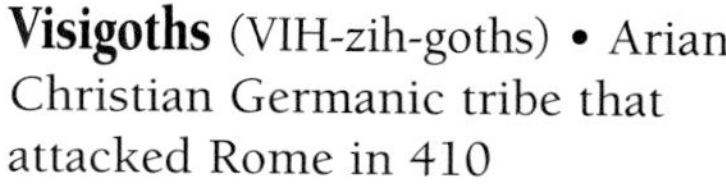

Visigoths (VIH-zih-goths) • Arian Christian Germanic tribe that attacked Rome in 410

von Bingen (fon-BIN-gen), **Hildegard** (HIL-duh-gard), 1098–1179 • Benedictine abbess and mystic

William, 1027–1087 • Duke of Normandy who claimed the English throne in 1066; led the Norman conquest of England

Wycliffe (WHY-klif), **John,** 1324–1384 • Oxford professor and priest who wanted people to read the Bible in their own language

SOME PRONUNCIATIONS

Aachen (AH-ken)

Anjou (AHN-joo)

Avignon (ah-vee-NYON)

Bologna (boh-LONE-ya)

Dnieper (NEE-per) River

Kiev (KEY-ev)

Muscovy (MUS-kov-ee)

Neapolis (nee-A-puh-lis)

Novgorod (NOHV-gah-rod)

Poitiers (pwah-TYAY)

Pyrenees (PIR-ah-neez)

Ravenna (rah-VEH-nah)

Rouen (ruh-AHN)

Seville (suh-VIL)

Sicily (SIS-uh-lee)

THE EUROPEAN WORLD, 400–1450

Scandinavian
Peninsula
Y
Novgorod
Volga River
Baltic Sea
POLAND
MUSCOVY
Kiev
Dnieper River
ASIA
OPE
Danube River
HUNGARY
Venice
Ravenna
na
ITALY
Balkan
Peninsula
Constantinople
Rome
Naples
ANATOLIA
Sicily
Antioch
SYRIA
thage
Mediterranean Sea
Jerusalem
EGYPT

INTRODUCTION

WHAT WERE THE MIDDLE AGES IN THE MIDDLE *OF*?

Fourteenth-century historians divided history into three main eras. One era was in the distant past, the ancient Classical age of Greece and Rome. Another era was the historians' own "modern" time in the 14th century, the dawn of a new age of learning and art that later came to be called the Renaissance. Sandwiched between the Classical era and the Renaissance, from about 400 to 1450, was the medieval, or middle, time. Renaissance historians began to call that middle period the Middle Ages or the Dark Ages, because they thought it was a time of superstition, ignorance, and barbarism.

The term "Middle Ages" was created in the 14th century, just when the Middle Ages themselves were ending. Europeans of the Middle Ages didn't think of themselves as living in the middle of anything, or as living in any particular era. For them, history was not divided into separate periods. Instead, they regarded the past as a continuous procession of events from the biblical creation down to their own time. Wars and other big events, such as the formation of empires and kingdoms, were pieces of a pageant that began with creation and would continue to the end of the world.

In some ways, the modern historian's view of history is similar to the medieval view. Modern scholars see that the

Cheek pieces and a chain-mail neck guard are hinged to the frame of this Frankish helmet found in a warrior's grave at Morken, Germany. The nose guard has been broken off, probably in battle.

medieval world developed from the ancient world, and they see no complete break between the Middle Ages and the Renaissance. It is extremely hard, historians now realize, to find a clear dividing line between two historical periods. People did not wake up one morning at the dawn of the Middle Ages, or the end of the Middle Ages, and say, "I am living in a whole new era." For most people, daily life changed very little, even when a new king came to the throne or a battle was fought far away.

Medieval Europeans didn't think of themselves as medieval, and they didn't think of themselves as Europeans either. Unlike the term "Middle Ages," the word "Europe" is very old. It was inherited from the ancient geographers of classical Greece and Rome. To the classical geographers, Europe—whose name comes from Europa, a woman in an ancient Greek legend—was the continent that included Greece and Italy. Between Europe and the large landmass of Asia, geographers traced a boundary line through seas and along rivers. The boundary began in the Aegean Sea, between Greece and present-day Turkey, then ran north through the Black Sea and along the Don River west of the Ural Mountains in what is now the Ukraine. West of this line was Europe; east was Asia.

The waterways of Europe were more than boundaries. In medieval times, they were vital to transportation, especially in regions where the roads had fallen apart or the Romans had never built roads. People moved heavy loads, such as stones for building castles and churches, grain, barrels of wine, and kegs of salted fish, by water. Despite the danger of pirates, traders braved the Mediterranean Sea, which was a major route between the east and west, as it had been since ancient times. In northern Europe, the Baltic Sea united Russia with Scandinavia, Germany, England, and the Netherlands. The Atlantic Ocean was much more difficult and dangerous to navigate than the inland seas, but Europeans did develop a north-south shipping trade along the Atlantic coast. Rivers such as the Rhine and the Danube, which ran through much of central Europe, carried both passengers and cargo. On Europe's eastern edge, the Swedes traded along the Vistula and Dnieper Rivers to the Black Sea. Travel along all these waterways knitted the many peoples of Europe together.

On land, two major mountain ranges blocked the movement of people and goods. The Pyrenees separate the Iberian Peninsula—which today is shared by the nations of Spain and Portugal—from the rest of Europe. The snow-covered Alps stand like a wall between the Italian Peninsula and the rest of Europe. But migrating tribes, armies, and goods traveled through passes, which cut through both mountain ranges.

Without natural barriers for protection, Europe experienced many invasions and migrations in the early Middle Ages. Whole peoples moved across the landscape—sometimes taking generations to migrate to a new home, at other times advancing as swiftly as an army on horseback. As they moved, they encountered different soils and climates. The warmer, drier, and hillier south produced olives (a source of oil), grapes for wine, and figs, citrus fruits, and dates. Southern Europeans also grew wheat, particularly in the sandy soils of coastal areas and river valleys, which were easy to till with simple plows, and tended hardy sheep and goats.

Cooler, rainier northern Europe was more heavily forested, but there were grasslands and lush pasture for cattle, too. Grains such as wheat, rye, and barley grew well in the rich soil. The regional differences in climate and agriculture were reflected in what people drank and ate—beer and butter in the north, wine and olive oil in the south.

A Visigoth wore this eagle-shaped fibula, a clasp used to fasten a cloak, in the 6th century in Spain. The Visigoths, the western branch of the Goth tribe, invaded the Roman Empire in the late 4th century and settled in France and Spain.

However, medieval scholars didn't write about "northern Europe" and "southern Europe." Often they did not even give names to the countries we now know as France, Greece, Germany, Turkey, and Italy. They were more likely to group people by religion—Christians, Jews, and Muslims—than by nationality. Ordinary people didn't identify themselves by nationality, either. They might identify themselves through the names of their fathers or mothers—"I am Alfred, son of John"—or by the village or city in which they lived, or by a nickname given to them by their neighbors. People generally had only one name—last names were not common until the 14th century. In medieval Europe, most people's horizons were close to home, and the world was an intimate place.

A French farmer sharpens his scythe on a whetstone in this relief sculpture on Notre Dame Cathedral in Paris, which was completed in 1257. A farmer on a cathedral wall indicates the importance of agriculture in the medieval world.

CHAPTER 1

BELIEVERS AND BARBARIANS

THE END OF THE ROMAN EMPIRE

In the 4th century CE, the Roman Empire was beginning to collapse—although most Romans, including a young man named Augustine and his family, didn't yet realize it. Augustine lived from 354 to 430 CE, in a time when the world around him changed dramatically.

Augustine was born in Rome's North Africa province, where his family was well known and important. Augustine's father accepted the traditional Roman gods, many of them adopted from the Greeks. His mother, however, was a Christian who urged Augustine to worship the one God of the Jews and Christians. The split of beliefs in Augustine's home mirrored the growing division between traditional believers and Christians throughout the empire. This division would define the world that took shape after Rome fell.

Like other Roman boys of his class, Augustine learned Latin and Greek and read stories of the ancient gods, goddesses, and heroes. His parents expected that he would one day hold a position in the Roman imperial government. So when he was in his teens they sent him to the North African city of Carthage to learn about literature, geometry, philosophy, and rhetoric—the art of making convincing arguments. Augustine would also have studied Rome's history.

At its origin, centuries before Augustine's birth, the Roman state controlled only the city of Rome and the surrounding countryside. Over time it conquered parts of Europe, North Africa, and western Asia. At the height of the empire, the Romans ruled a vast territory and many peoples, including Celts in Britain, France, and Spain; Berbers and Egyptians in North Africa; Germanic tribes in what is now Germany; and Greeks, Syrians, Jews, and Arabs on

The Making of a Martyr

A ROMAN EYEWITNESS, ACCOUNT OF VIBIA PERPETUA'S DEATH, 203

Augustine's mother was not the only Roman woman who embraced Christianity. Many did so. One of them was Vibia Perpetua, the daughter of a high-ranking Roman official. Vibia Perpetua refused to renounce her Christianity. She wrote an account of her arrest, her father's anguish, how she cared for her infant son in prison, and her visions of deliverance into heaven. A contemporary eyewitness had to write the end of her story because she died in an arena in Carthage on March 7, 203, with a fellow martyr named Felicity.

Now dawned the day of their victory, and they went forth from the prison into the amphitheater as it were into heaven, cheerful and bright of countenance; if they trembled at all, it was for joy, not for fear. Perpetua followed behind [Felicity] glorious of presence, as a true spouse of Christ and darling of God; at whose piercing look all cast down their eyes. . . .

Roman soldiers brutally killed Perpetua for refusing to renounce her Christian faith.

But for the women [was] prepared a most ferocious heifer. . . . Perpetua was first tossed by the heifer, and fell on her loins. But then she sat up and pulled down her tunic—that was torn along the side—to cover her thighs, more mindful of her modesty than of her pain. Next she asked for a pin and fastened her untidy hair. For it was not right for a martyr to die with disheveled hair, that in her hour of glory she might not appear to be in mourning. Then she rose, and seeing that Felicity had been dashed to the ground, she went to her, gave her hand, and raised her up. Now the two were side by side. They had overcome the cruelty of the mob and were called back through the Gate of Life. There Perpetua . . . as now awakening from sleep (so much was she in the Spirit and in ecstasy) began first to look about her. . . . When, forsooth, quoth she, are we to be thrown to the cow? And when she heard that this had been done already, she would not believe till she perceived some marks of mauling on her body and on her dress. Thereupon she called her brother to her . . . saying: Stand fast in the faith, and love ye all one another.

Crowds gathered in this late-1st-century amphitheater to watch chariot races and to cheer gladiators in their life-and-death battles against each other and ferocious animals. Arenas such as this one in Arles, France, dotted the Roman Empire, which stretched across North Africa and Europe and east into Asia.

eastern Mediterranean shores. By Augustine's time, the empire was like a huge doughnut with the Mediterranean Sea in its hole. From east to west it extended three thousand miles, approximately the distance between New York City and San Francisco.

Rome couldn't defend its long border from all its invaders. And within the empire, rebellions made politics so stormy that many emperors were murdered. Economic and social conditions worsened because the Roman economy relied on slaves to grow food and make goods. When the empire stopped expanding, its supply of slaves diminished, and Rome's prosperity shrank. Its great public works, such as roads, bathhouses, and aqueducts carrying fresh water to cities, suffered from neglect.

But perhaps Rome's greatest weakness was in its army. The army was no longer made up of Roman citizens, as in the old days. Instead, its ranks were filled with foreigners who didn't know much about Rome's laws, customs, and way of life. Some did not even speak Latin, the language of Rome. Generals recruited soldiers from tribes on the borders of the empire, promising them pay and even land in exchange for fighting. These foreign soldiers were loyal only for pay.

The young Augustine observed these matters from a distance. He was away from home, studying and enjoying himself like a typical upper-class Roman teenager. When he was 18, he took a mistress, with whom he had a son. Ambitious to play a major role in Roman politics, Augustine moved to Milan, Italy. After becoming engaged to a wealthy young woman of his own class, he cast aside his mistress and their son. While in Milan, however, Augustine did something else—something that would have a lasting effect on him. He heard the sermons of Ambrose, a powerful Christian bishop. Ambrose, who was known as the Honey-Tongued Doctor for his persuasive preaching, excommunicated the Roman emperor Theodosius for having massacred the population of Thessalonica, an ancient city in Macedonia: "You [Theodosius] have a tremendous zeal for the Christian faith . . . but you also have an exceedingly violent temper. . . . I did repeatedly denounce it [the massacre] at court as an atrocity. . . . I advise you . . . to repent."

The iron boss, or bump, on the outside of this round, wooden shield protected the hand of the tribal warrior, who held his shield by a central grip on the inside as he plunged into battle.

Christianity was causing turmoil in the Roman Empire. It had been spreading since the 1st century CE, when the original followers of Jesus spoke in markets and public places, encouraging people to become Christians. Soon believers were meeting in small congregations led by Christian clergy. As the religion spread, so did official concern and suspicion. Roman

The young Roman nobleman Augustine (center) arrives in Milan to meet the Christian bishop Ambrose (far right). Augustine was so moved by the bishop's sermons that he converted to Christianity and spent his life writing and preaching about his religious beliefs.

authorities feared that Christianity could be politically dangerous, causing uprisings against the empire. They particularly feared the growing popularity of Christianity among groups who were likely to rebel: the poor in the cities, slaves, and even soldiers. In the early 4th century, one emperor tried to end the threat by ordering the seizure of Christian books and the execution of Christians who would not give up their faith. Some Christians obeyed, turning over their books and renouncing their religion. Others, though, became martyrs, believers who suffered torture and death for their faith.

Such punishments probably strengthened Christianity by impressing the crowds with the force of the martyrs' beliefs. But the real boost to Christianity came when an emperor named Constantine converted to the faith. Constantine's father was the junior emperor in charge of the empire's westernmost provinces. His mother was a Christian, who went to Jerusalem and supposedly discovered the site of Jesus' tomb. To make sure that Constantine's father remained loyal, the senior emperor kept Constantine as a hostage in his eastern court. After his father's death, Constantine escaped, traveling on horses stationed at post stops to carry mail to the West.

Terrified of being followed, Constantine crippled each horse by cutting its leg tendons after he arrived at a new post. Once in the West, he raised an army to fight the other rivals to his father's throne.

In 312, on the eve of a battle that would make him ruler of the whole empire, Constantine dreamed he heard the words "*In hoc vinci*" (In this sign you will conquer). The next day he saw the sign, a circle with a cross in it, in the heavens. Constantine's biographer, Eusebius, who knew him personally, wrote that Constantine "doubted within himself what the [meaning] of this apparition could be.... In his sleep the Christ of God appeared to him with the same sign he had seen in the heavens, and [instructed him] to use it as a safeguard in all engagements with his enemies." He won the battle, accepted Christianity, and ended the empire's persecution of Christians.

Following Constantine's lead, many people of all classes converted to Christianity. The surge of new converts brought problems, however. Some of them—including Constantine himself—didn't understand the religion very well. Others were convinced that only their own interpretation was correct. One early dispute was about whether Jesus was divine or human. One group, followers of a monk called Arius, claimed that Jesus was human. Others argued that he was divine, while still others said that he was both. Tempers ran so high over the issue that fights broke out in the streets.

Tired of the civil unrest, Constantine called a council of bishops in 325 to decide the question. The council proclaimed, "We believe in one God, the Father Almighty,

Both an emperor and a religious leader, Constantine gave this official order in 313: "We decided that of the things that are of profit to all mankind, the worship of God ought rightly to be our first and chiefest care and that Christians and all others should have freedom to follow the kind of religion they favored."

maker of all things visible and invisible; and in one Lord Jesus Christ, the Son of God, the only-begotten of his Father, of the substance of the Father." In other words, God was the only divinity, and Jesus was part of God. The council declared the Arians to be heretics because they believed a heresy, an opinion that went against the church. Arianism did not die out at once, however. Missionaries had converted tribes outside the empire to the Arian version of Christianity. When those peoples entered the empire, they were set apart from the Romans not just by their different languages and customs but also by their form of Christianity.

Even after Constantine converted, Christianity did not immediately replace the old Roman gods and become the official religion of the Roman Empire. One of Constantine's most important actions, however, shaped the future of the Christian faith. In 330 the emperor moved the capital from Rome to Byzantium, a small Greek city near Asia Minor, or present-day Turkey. He renamed it Constantinople after himself and urged senators and noble families to move there from Rome. After that move, the empire was gradually divided into two parts.

The Eastern, or Byzantine, Empire consisted of Greece, Asia Minor, and the eastern Mediterranean. The Western Empire included the rest of Europe and the western Mediterranean. As the division became more permanent, each part developed its own version of Christianity. Eventually these would become Orthodox Christianity in the East and Roman Catholicism in the West. At first, Christianity spread more rapidly in the Eastern Empire than in the Western. Still, many western Romans were drawn to the faith by eloquent speakers such as Ambrose, the bishop who preached to Augustine in Milan. Ambrose's powers of persuasion come through in such letters as this: "The Church's foundation is unshakable and firm against assaults of the raging sea. Waves lash at the Church but do not shatter it. Although the elements of this world constantly beat upon the Church with crashing sounds, the Church possesses the safest harbor of salvation for all in distress."

Deeply moved by Ambrose's sermons, Augustine felt increasingly guilty about his life of sensual pleasure and his political ambition. Torn between traditional belief in the Roman gods and the Christian faith of his mother and Bishop Ambrose, he was confused. In his autobiography *Confessions,* Augustine described how one day, while weeping in his garden, he heard a child's voice say, "Take it and read." He opened the New Testament to this passage: "Not in rioting or drunkenness, not in . . . wantonness, not in strife

Early Christian churches were built on the model of Roman secular buildings. This picture of Constantine's basilica shows how grand these could be.

and envying, but put on the Lord Jesus Christ, and make no provision for the flesh to fulfill the lusts thereof."

"As I finished the sentence, as though the light of peace had been poured into my heart, and all the shadows of doubt dispersed," Augustine wrote later in *Confessions*. He went into his house and told his mother, who was overjoyed. His decision was made. He converted to Christianity and settled in the North African city of Hippo, where he eventually became bishop—a career very different from the one he had originally planned for himself.

BARBARIANS AT THE GATES!

The empire was changing, too. The economy kept growing weaker, and the army could no longer defend the frontiers. Most vulnerable was the long northern frontier, which roughly followed the Rhine and Danube Rivers. South and west of the rivers lay the empire: the Roman part of Europe, consisting of present-day France, Spain, and Italy. But to the north and east were the foreign lands that are now Germany, Scandinavia, Austria, the Czech Republic, and Hungary. Tribes of people known to historians as Germans and Goths occupied these lands. Greeks and Romans, however, called them barbarians because they thought the Germanic languages sounded like "bar, bar, bar."

The women and slaves of the Germanic tribes were farmers, but the men were hunters, plunderers, and warriors who gathered in bands around war chiefs. These aggressive fighters could easily cross the rivers into Roman territory. Their values and way of life differed greatly from those of the Romans. Mediterranean civilization was based on cities and agriculture; the invaders preferred rural areas and hunting. Roman government was centralized and highly organized; the tribes were organized loosely around kings, fighting bands, and family groups. Roman society was highly literate; the tribespeople were illiterate. Finally, Romans valued their public and private baths, but the Germans were, to Roman nostrils, a dirty and smelly group. A priest from Marseilles, France, wrote in about 440, that the Romans "share none of [the barbarians'] manners or their speech, and . . . Nothing, furthermore, of the fetid odor of the barbarians' bodies and clothes."

Some tribespeople learned Roman ways and moved their families peacefully into areas of the empire the Romans had abandoned. Still, many Germanic tribes kept their own languages and traditional laws. As the tribes mingled with the Romans, they added a few new twists to their old rules. One law of the Franks, a Germanic people who invaded northern Gaul, or France, said, "If anyone has assaulted and plundered a free person, and it be proved upon him, he shall be [fined] 2,500 dinars, which make 63 shillings. If a Roman has plundered a Frank, the above law shall be observed. But if a Frank has plundered a Roman, he shall be [fined] 35 shillings." To the Franks, it seems, a crime against a Roman was about half as serious as a crime against one of their own kind.

The Germanic migration into the empire gained speed and urgency when a new threat arrived in the late fourth century. The Huns, nomads who traveled on horseback, were originally from central Asia. When drought ruined their pastures, they moved west seeking better conditions for their livestock—and themselves. Both the Romans and the Germanic tribes viewed the Huns with dread. One observer, a Goth named Jordanes, described the invaders as "small, foul and skinny; their faces were seamed with gashes, their noses broad and flat. They dressed in coarse linen tunics, which they never changed until they rotted; on their heads they wore a sort of helmet made with skins of wild rats patched together."

The advance of the Huns forced the Germanic tribes east of the Danube into motion. A group called the Visigoths, or West Goths, who were already Arian Christians, asked the Byzantine emperor for permission to settle in the Balkan Peninsula, a mountainous region south of the Danube River with Greece at its southern point. The emperor granted

This small gold statue of a warrior probably represents a member of the Frankish tribe that began invading northern Gaul (later called France) in the late 4th century.

An ornately carved scene of brutal hand-to-hand combat between Romans and Germanic tribes decorates the sarcophagus, or stone coffin, of a Roman soldier.

permission, thinking that the Visigoths would be a useful buffer between his empire and the Huns. But when the emperor failed to pay the Visigoths the money he had promised them for fighting, their king led them west, into Italy.

As the Visigoths advanced on Rome in 410, the young western emperor panicked and fled, leaving the city open to the invaders. Under their king, Alaric, the Visigoths plundered the city and then moved south with their loot and hostages—including Galla Placidia, the emperor's sister. When Alaric died, his followers feared the Romans would dishonor his grave because they hated him so much. Legend holds that the Visigoths diverted a stream and had captives bury Alaric's body under its bed. They then killed the captives and redirected the stream over Alaric's grave. To this day, no one knows where Alaric lies buried.

The Visigoths chose a new king, Athaulf, who led them into Spain. Athaulf married Galla Placidia, whose lavish wedding gifts were probably stolen from Rome. But Galla Placidia was no weak victim. Tradition says that she agreed to the marriage and persuaded her husband to defend, rather than continue to attack, the empire. But in Spain Athaulf was murdered by one of his own men. His widow returned to Rome and married a Roman. She concluded her eventful life by ruling in the name of her infant son, who was made emperor.

The image of Rome sacked and overrun by Visigoths haunted citizens of the empire. And Rome's problems continued. The Huns, not content with harassing the Germanic tribes, turned their attention to richer prey. Their leader from 433 to 453 was Attila, whose reputation for brutality had earned him the nickname the "Scourge of Europe."

Attila had his sights set on Rome. An army of Romans and Visigoths fighting together forced Attila to retreat, but within a year he was plundering his way toward Rome once again. Only the city's bishop stood in his way, offering him gifts if he would leave. Again Attila retreated, this time most likely because of plague in his army. Taking yet another wife to join the many he already had, he died on his wedding night, perhaps of too much food and drink. Even after

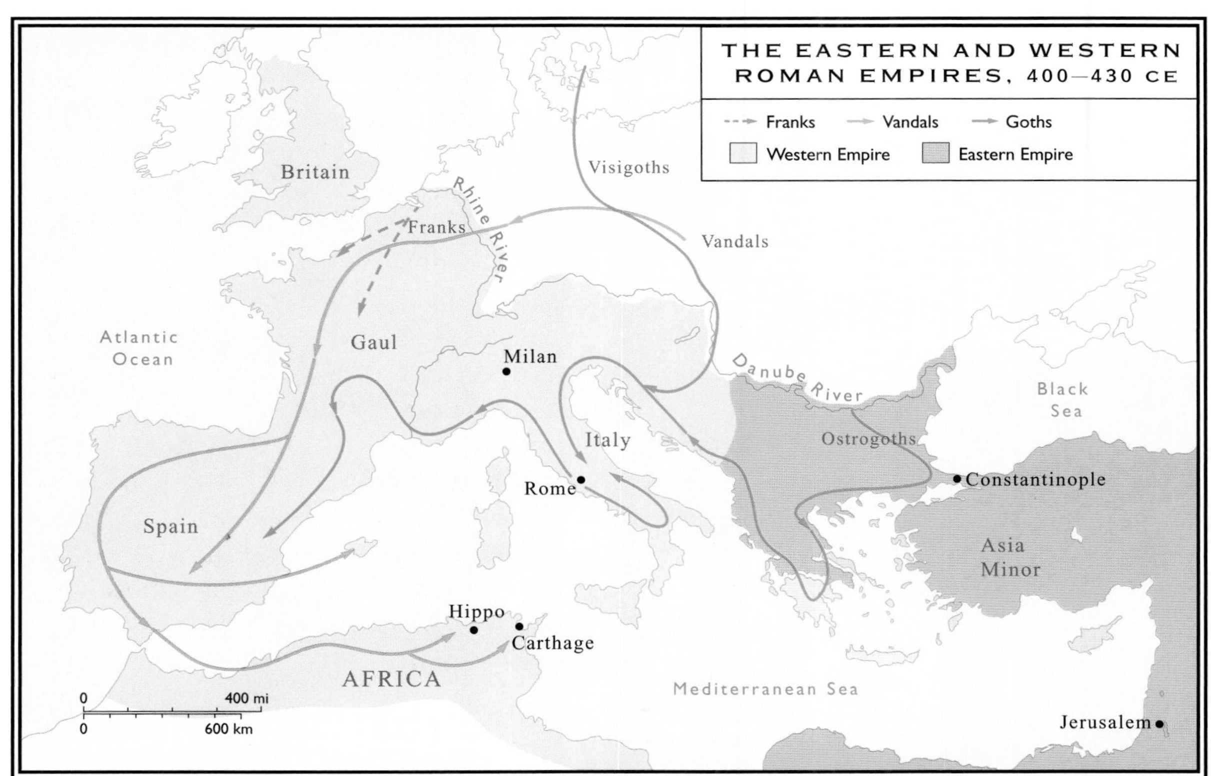

Attila's death, unrest stirred up by the Huns sparked new migrations and invasions of Germanic peoples.

Augustine, following his religious path in the North African city of Hippo, heard all the news. He and other citizens of the far-flung empire now realized that barbarian tribes could cross the imperial borders almost at will. He knew that they had sacked the city of Rome and that a centuries-old way of life was ending. Yet Augustine did not despair at the changes in his world. In *The City of God,* a book of religious thought, he wrote that the world of the spirit was more important than that of the empire. "The city of the ungodly... is void of true justice," he wrote. Still, worldly changes pressed close to home for Augustine when another Germanic tribe, the Vandals, set up a kingdom in Carthage, in North Africa. Just months after Augustine's death, Hippo fell to the Vandals.

Augustine lived in a turbulent era. People had to struggle with conflicting beliefs, adjust to different forms of government, learn new languages, and cope with violence. The

The carvings on this stone coffin from the 4th century are symbols of the Christian religion. The fish stands for people who have joined the faith, the anchor signifies hope, and the shepherd and sheep represent Christ caring for his flock.

"The tribes of Germany... appear as a distinct, unmixed race, like none but themselves.... All have fierce blue eyes, red hair, huge frames, fit only for a sudden exertion."

—Tacitus, *Germania*, 98

turmoil came from clashes among three cultures: Roman, Christian, and barbarian. These three cultures had shaped Augustine's world, and they would shape the next era of European civilization, the Middle Ages.

Latin, the language of learning, came from Roman culture. Rome's legacy also lived on in many of the laws and government structures that emerged in the medieval period. The physical remains of Rome—walls, roads, bridges, aqueducts, stadiums, temples, and even some private homes—not only dotted the landscape of Europe but in some cases remained in use through the Middle Ages.

To this Roman base, Christianity brought new spiritual values and a unifying religion. It inspired medieval art, literature, and architecture. Just as the child Augustine had heard tales of the ancient gods and heroes, children of the Middle Ages heard stories of the Christian martyrs and saints—including Augustine, who was made a saint of the Roman Catholic Church. And Germanic languages, laws, and customs blended with Roman ones, as the Germans and Romans merged to form the new population of Europe.

CHAPTER 2

SURROUNDED BY "A SEA OF TRIBES"

EUROPE BECOMES CHRISTIAN

Sidonius Apollinaris was a Roman man of high social status—so high that he married the emperor's daughter. And like other high-ranking Romans, he served the church as earlier generations of Romans had served the imperial government, administering civic services as well as spiritual comfort. As bishop in Clermont in what is now central France, Sidonius was responsible for organizing the city's defense

In this relief sculpture, dating from the 7th century, a bearded Frankish warrior rides bareback and carries a spear and shield. The Franks fought on horseback, riding without saddles, but the warrior is using a bridle and reins.

against the Visigoths who attacked it in the 470s. His letters reveal the meeting and mingling of Germans and Romans, pagans and Christians in the early Middle Ages. In a letter to a friend, he wrote, "Our own town lives in terror of a sea of tribes which find in it an obstacle to their expansion and surge in arms all around it." When Clermont fell to the Visigoths, Sidonius spent three years as their prisoner.

Yet the tribes, Sidonius noted, were changing. Describing the Germanic prince Sigismer and his army in a letter to a friend, Sidonius explained the differences between a somewhat Roman German and the other "barbarians." Wrote Sidonius,

> With charming modesty [Sigismer] went afoot amid his body guards and footmen, in flame-red mantle, with much glint of ruddy gold, and gleam of snowy silken tunic, his fair hair, red cheeks and white skin according with the three hues of his equipment. But the chiefs and allies who bore him company were dread of aspect.... Their feet were laced in boots of bristly hide reaching to the heels; ankles and legs were exposed. They wore tight tunics of varied color hardly descending to their bare knees, the sleeves covering only the upper arms.

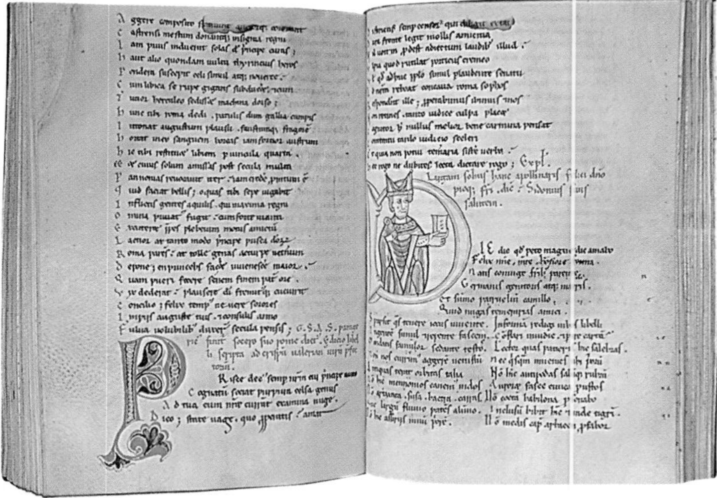

The Roman bishop Sidonius Apollinaris wrote his poems and letters in Latin. "The Latin language stands unshaken," he wrote to a friend. As the barbarians invaded, though, their languages spread throughout the Roman Empire. By the late 5th century, Latin only survived within the Catholic Church.

Although Sidonius lived far from Rome, to him Rome remained the center of civilization. He called it, when writing to a Roman friend, "the abode of law, the training-school of letters, the font of honors, the head of the world, the motherland of freedom, the city unique upon earth where none but the barbarian and slave is foreign."

But he knew that the Roman world was changing around him, and he looked to Christianity to preserve learning and bring civilization to the barbarians.

This iron and gold crown with precious stones was worn by a Lombardy queen named Theodelinda. The Lombards were a tough, proud people who resisted conversion to Christianity.

Christianity didn't always unify people, however. Many of the Germanic tribes had converted to the Arian form of Christianity. At first they were hostile to people who followed Roman Christianity, although eventually they too accepted that Jesus was divine. But another tribe, the Franks, still worshipped their old gods and knew little about Christianity. After the Franks moved into France, a Christian woman named Clotilda gave their history a new direction. Clotilda married the pagan king of the Franks and launched one of the great ruling families of early medieval Europe.

LET'S BE FRANK

Clotilda's uncle, a Germanic king, had murdered her father and drowned her mother by tying a stone around her neck. Her sister retreated to a home for Christian nuns. Clotilda might have done the same, but her beauty impressed Clovis, king of the Franks. Clovis married Clotilda, who immediately began trying to convert him to Christianity. She persuaded him to allow their first two sons to be baptized, but because they died in infancy, their father remained unconvinced of the new religion's worth. Finally, as Gregory of Tours, a French bishop of Roman descent, wrote in *The History of the Franks*, Clovis, about to be slaughtered by enemy troops, "raised his hands fervently toward the heavens and, breaking into tears, cried: 'Jesus Christ . . . I invoke thy marvelous help. If thou wilt give me victory over my enemies, . . . I will believe in thee and will be baptized in thy name.'" After his victory, he and his army were baptized. Although Clovis knew little about his new faith, he now considered himself a Roman Christian. The pope later called on the Franks for help against pagan invaders of Italy. Clovis unified the Franks and established a dynasty called the Merovingians after a mythical ancestor called Meroweg. Unifying the Frankish kingdom, however, was no easy matter. The Franks passed property from one generation to the next by dividing a father's lands and possessions equally among his sons. When a man died, his sons would fight among themselves until one dominated. If ordinary people fought over inheritances—and they did—imagine how fiercely brothers battled one another over a kingdom. Clovis himself had come to power after many battles in which his close relatives were killed. Bishop Gregory of Tours wrote in his *History of the Franks* that Clovis once said to a large group of Franks, "Oh woe is me, for I travel among strangers and have none of my kinsfolk to help me!" But Gregory suggested that perhaps Clovis "did not refer to their deaths out of grief, but craftily, to see if he could bring to light some new relatives to kill."

A bishop pours water over the head of Clovis in this 14th-century manuscript showing the baptism of the Frankish king. His conversion helped Christianity to gain power in Europe.

In spite of their infighting, the Franks became a strong power in Europe. They encouraged missionaries to convert their family and friends to Christianity in the lands across the Rhine River that are now modern Germany. A pagan group called the Lombards, who had moved from Germany into northern Italy, were among the most difficult to convert. A story about a Lombard king and his queen reveals the tribe's brutal ways. The king killed his wife's father, a rival chieftain. Proud of his deed, he carried his father-in-law's skull about as a trophy. During a banquet, he filled the skull with wine and forced his wife to drink to his health. She obeyed, but she also vowed to murder her husband—a promise she kept. Yet eventually the Lombards, too, became Christians.

As the Germanic tribes settled in Europe, they wrote laws to keep the Roman and Germanic populations apart, but it was impossible to keep them separate. Romans and Germans intermarried. Languages blended and evolved to create Italian, French, Spanish, and Romanian. These are called Romance languages because they are based on the Roman language, Latin.

PAPA AND THE VENERABLE BEDE

A shared culture—customs, traditions, and beliefs practiced by both Roman and Germanic populations—gradually emerged in Europe. The church kept alive many Roman elements of that culture. Latin was the language used in church services and documents. The church also provided leadership. Since the early days of Christianity, bishops had led congregations and communities. Their religious duties included ordaining priests, or formally granting them the power to conduct rites, and then supervising their conduct; overseeing Christian teaching; and regulating monasteries. In the early Middle Ages, bishops became town leaders as well. Like Sidonius, they governed towns and the countryside around them.

Cathedrals, the churches led by bishops, were at the center of both worship and civic administration. Some were quite grand. Describing a cathedral built in Clermont-Ferrand,

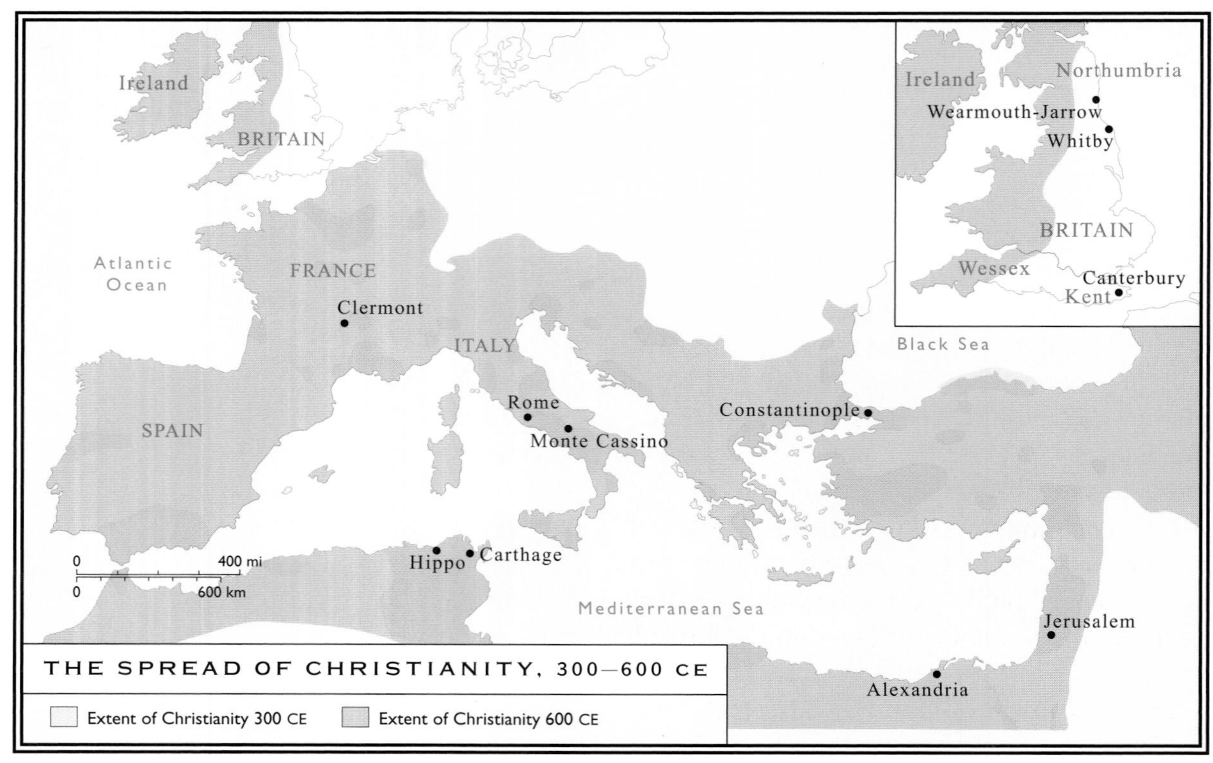

THE SPREAD OF CHRISTIANITY, 300–600 CE

France, Bishop Gregory of Tours wrote, "The whole building is constructed in the shape of a cross. It has fifty-two windows, seventy columns and eight doorways. In it one is conscious of the fear of God and of a great brightness."

The highest-ranking bishop in western Europe was the bishop of Rome. Christian tradition said that Peter, one of Jesus' original followers, had founded the first church in Rome before being martyred there. As Peter's successor, the bishop of Rome was considered the head of the church. He came to be called pope or *papa*, which is Latin for "father." Rome was the old imperial capital, and people were used to looking to the city and its government for guidance. The able men in Rome who held the papacy, or office of the pope, gave it great stature. Among them were heroic leaders such as Pope Gregory the Great, who promoted missionary activity to spread Christianity in the 6th century, declaring that even the Anglo-Saxon slave children "have the face of angels, and... should be fellow-heirs of the angels in heaven."

Peter, one of Jesus' followers, was thought to have founded the first Christian church in Rome. According to the New Testament, Jesus said to Peter, "I will give you the keys to the kingdom of heaven." This is the reason medieval illustrations, such as this one from Italy, always show him carrying two keys.

As Christianity advanced within the old empire, people on the fringes remained pagan. A number of medieval monks became missionaries to carry the faith to them. One was Saint Patrick, who converted the Irish in the early 6th century. According to his early biographer, Patrick came from a Christian family in Britain, but Irish raiders captured him when he was 16. He spent six miserable years as a slave in Ireland before he escaped and returned to Britain. A dream told him to return to Ireland and convert the people to Christianity, and he accepted the mission. Many of Patrick's followers were killed, and he was nearly martyred, but Ireland became Christian. The Irish then sent their own missionaries to northern England, where their monasteries preserved Latin learning and converted the local people. Unlike monasteries in other parts of Europe, those of northern England housed both men and women and were often supervised by abbesses rather than abbots.

Another form of monastic life, created by a young Roman nobleman, came from Italy. Born in Nursia, near Spoleto, around 480, Benedict didn't follow the usual career path for his class. Instead of entering politics, he lived alone and devoted himself to prayer. His reputation as a holy man grew, and he gained followers—too many to settle near him. Benedict also saw that his disciples were overwhelmed by worldly temptations and that they fought with one another. To give them a more peaceful refuge, Benedict moved from near Rome to Monte Cassino in southern Italy. His sister, Scholastica, set up a convent nearby; she became the patron saint of Benedictine nuns.

Benedict wrote a set of rules for the monks who were his followers. The Benedictine Rule required three vows: poverty, chastity, and complete obedience to the abbot, the head of the monastery. When a person entered a monastery or nunnery, he or she gave all personal possessions to the community and wore simple robes and sandals. A new member went through a period of trial, called a novitiate, before taking the final vows. This gave novices a chance to be certain that they really wanted the rigors of monastic life. When novices took their final vows, they wore the symbols of their order. Men shaved their heads, leaving only a ring of hair called a tonsure. Women donned a veil.

Benedictine monks and nuns had responsibilities according to their skills. Some were administrators. Others copied manuscripts and decorated them with colorful images called illuminations. Others educated children, worked in the kitchens and barns, or became priests. Everyone prayed seven times a day—and, recognizing that it wasn't always easy to get up before sunrise to pray, the Benedictine Rule asked that brothers and sisters gently

"Let clothing be given to the brethren suitable to the nature and climate of the place where they live. . . . We think . . . a cowl and a tunic should suffice for each monk."

—Benedictine Rule, 6th century

Benedict (standing, center) and his sister, Scholastica, formed what is called the Benedictine Order within the Catholic Church. The monks and nuns behind them are wearing the simple robes of the order. The men shaved all but a ring of hair on their heads, and the women wore veils. In the upper right, angels help a Christian soul to Heaven.

encourage one another to do so. Their plain diet consisted of cheese, fish, bread, beans, and a good measure of wine every day, although the young, sick, and elderly could eat some meat for strength. Monastic buildings included a dormitory for sleeping, a large kitchen, storage areas, barns, a chapter house for meetings, a chapel, a scriptorium for writing and keeping books, and a cloister for meditation and growing medicinal herbs. The monks' and nuns' lives were simple, orderly, and dedicated to prayer, learning, and service to the poor.

One early follower of the Benedictine Rule was a young man who became Pope Gregory the Great. Like Benedict,

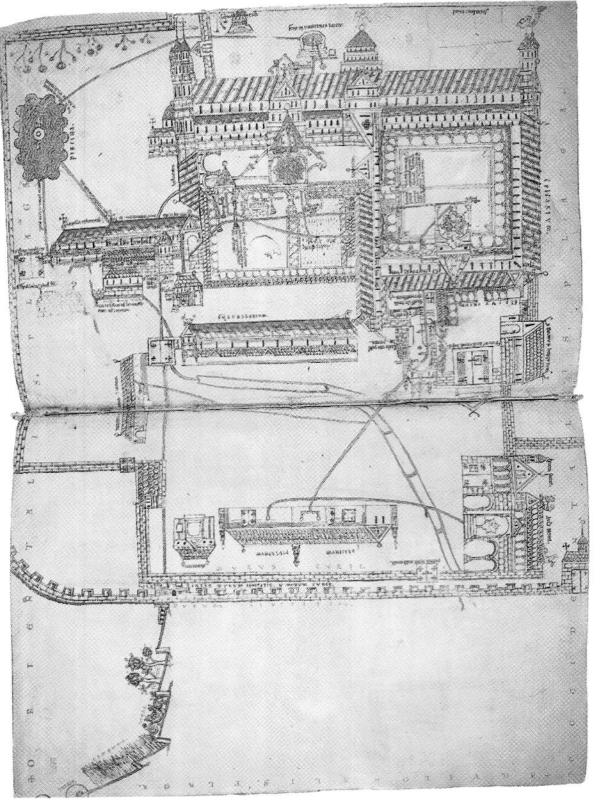

At the top of this plan for the Benedictine monastery at Canterbury, England, is Canterbury Cathedral. The two squares are the cloisters, open areas with arched corridors (shown as scalloped borders). Monks meditated here, and grew herbs in the garden of the central cloister. Monasteries were self-sufficient communities run according to very strict rules.

he came from a noble Roman family but preferred the monastic life. His lasting achievement as pope was to send Benedictine missionaries to spread Christianity in northern Europe. England became Christian partly because of Gregory's missionary efforts, but several remarkable women helped. They were descended from Clotilda, who had been made a saint for helping to convert her husband, Clovis, king of the Franks.

Clotilda's great-granddaughter Bertha married the king of Kent, one of the English kingdoms. Although the king let his wife bring a Christian priest to her new home, he continued to practice the pagan religion of his ancestors. Pope Gregory sent Bertha a bishop who succeeded in converting her husband and his followers. That bishop became known as Saint Augustine of Canterbury. England, however, was not yet completely Christian. Bertha's daughter Ethelberga married the king of Northumbria, in northern England, and converted him to Christianity, too.

Northern England was a problem for the church. Even after it became Christian, its Irish religious practices were quite different from Roman traditions. Irish monks celebrated Easter on a different date from the Romans, and they shaved their heads from ear to ear instead of leaving the tonsure. In 664 a synod, or church council, met at the monastery of Whitby in northern England to bring local practices into line with Roman traditions. The Irish representative reported that, "The Easter which I keep I received from my elders," to which the Roman representative replied that "the Picts and the Britons, . . . foolishly, in these two remote islands of the world, and only in part even of them, oppose all the rest of the universe. . . . " The Northumbrian king attended the synod and was confused by the theological arguments in favor of Roman practice. He decided on a simpler test and asked both sides if Peter had founded the Church of Rome. When both agreed, the king decided in favor of Roman practice.

England's new religious unity produced the most famous author of the late 7th and early 8th centuries, and the most learned man of his day. Bede, later called the Venerable Bede because of his learning, was a Benedictine monk who spent his life at the English monasteries of Wearmouth and Jarrow. He read all the manuscripts in their remarkable libraries and summed up the learning of his

A Benedictine monk copies a book. Before the invention of printing, manuscripts were painstakingly copied by hand and then bound into books. This was one of the important jobs of the monks, who also decorated the texts with tiny, intricate colored scenes called miniatures.

time in his own writings. His *Ecclesiastical History of the English People* tells of the Synod of Whitby and various political events; it also recounts the lives of kings, queens, abbots, abbesses, and saints.

By the end of the 7th century, the political and cultural map of Europe had changed greatly from the days of the old Roman Empire. Separate kingdoms were emerging all over western Europe. A Germanic people called the Anglo-Saxons ruled several kingdoms within England. The Franks had settled France. The Visigoths controlled Spain, and the Lombards had taken over northern Italy. The papacy was established in Rome and controlled the surrounding countryside. Northern Europe was splintered into smaller units, still following some tribal customs and ruled by kings. These northerners were officially Christian, but they held onto some of their old pagan practices, and a few of those customs have survived to the present—the names of the days Tuesday, Wednesday, and Thursday, for example, come from the names of the Germanic gods Tiu, Woden, and Thor.

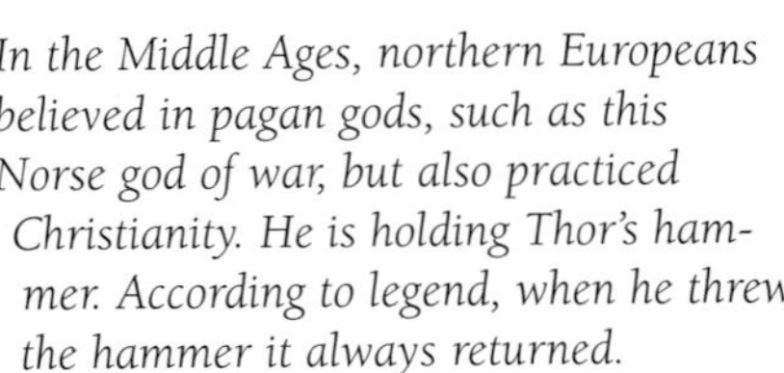

In the Middle Ages, northern Europeans believed in pagan gods, such as this Norse god of war, but also practiced Christianity. He is holding Thor's hammer. According to legend, when he threw the hammer it always returned.

Mysterious Deaths in Marseilles

GREGORY OF TOURS, HISTORY OF THE FRANKS, 6TH CENTURY

The Middle Ages began and ended with outbreaks of the deadly bubonic plague. The first plague struck Europe in the middle of the 6th century. Plague is an infection that spreads to humans bitten by fleas that have picked up bacteria from infected rats. Rats and fleas were both plentiful in the Middle Ages. The plague killed three-fourths of all those who became infected. Gregory of Tours, a Roman bishop living in France, wrote a History of the Franks *in the 6th century, which included this chronicle of the effects of the first plague and detailed account of its symptoms.*

The city of Marseilles was suffering from a most serious epidemic of swelling. I want to tell you exactly how this came about. . . . a ship from Spain put into port with the usual kind of cargo, unfortunately also bringing with it the source of infection. Quite a few of the townsfolk purchased objects from the cargo and in less than no time a house in which eight people lived was left completely deserted, all the inhabitants having caught the disease. The infection did not spread through the residential quarter immediately. Some time passed and then, like a cornfield set alight, the entire town was suddenly ablaze with the pestilence. For all that Bishop Theodore came back and took up residence in Saint Victor's church, together with seven poor folk who remained at his side. There he stayed throughout the whole of the catastrophe which assailed his city, giving up all his time to prayers and vigils, and imploring God in His mercy to put an end to the slaughter and to allow the people some peace and quiet. At the end of two months the plague burned itself out. The population returned to Marseilles, thinking themselves safe. Then the disease started again and all who had come back died. On several occasions later on Marseilles suffered from an epidemic of this sort.

Victims of the plague are buried in Tournai, Belgium, in 1349.

CHAPTER 3

THREE EMPIRES

JUSTINIAN, CHARLEMAGNE, AND MUHAMMAD

Three empires shaped the early Middle Ages. In the East, the Byzantine Empire carried the heritage of imperial Rome. In the West, a new dynasty turned the kingdom of the Franks into an empire. And in Arabia, a new religion called Islam became the unifying force of another empire. The history of these empires is woven from the strands of thousands of lives—including an ambitious husband and wife, a family who took over the French throne, and a caravan trader turned prophet.

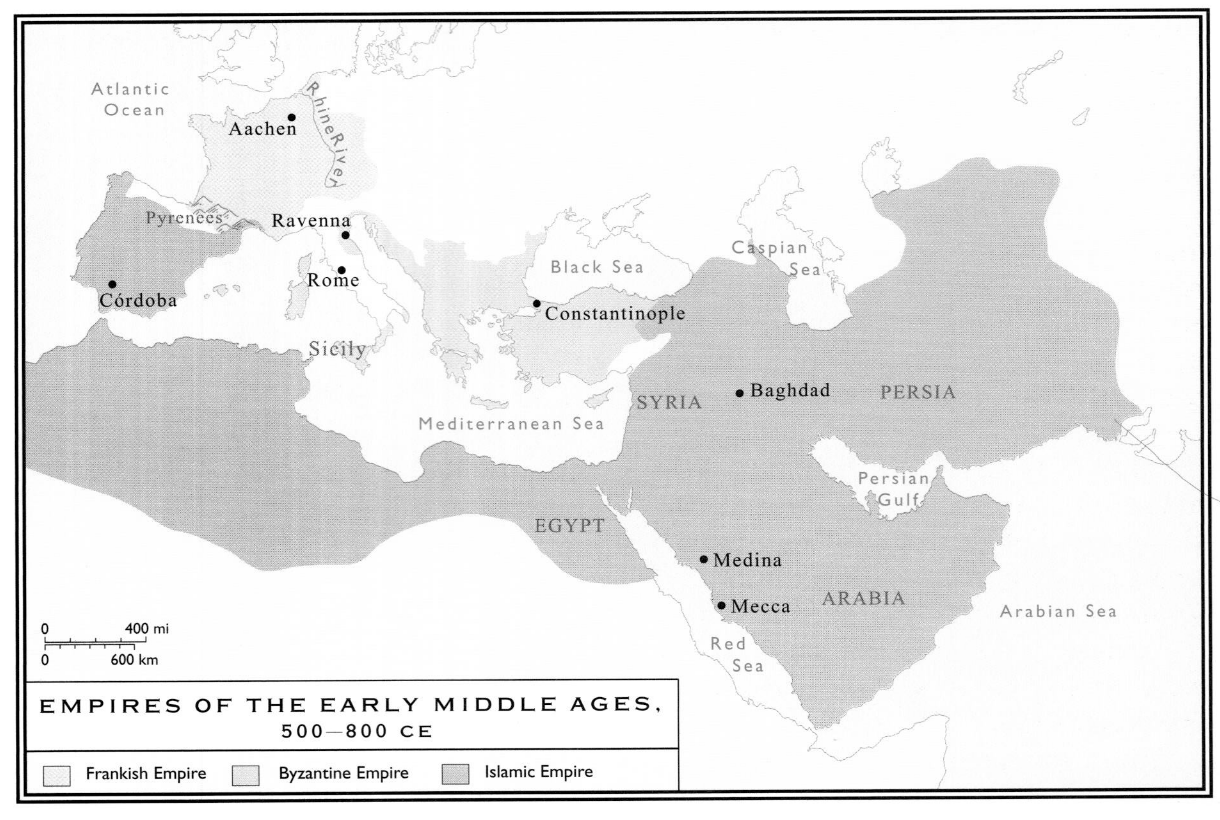

The husband and wife were Justinian and Theodora, emperor and empress of the Byzantines. During the 5th and 6th centuries, while tribes in the western part of the former Roman Empire fought among themselves, the rich, city-centered Byzantine Empire endured in the East. But the eastern emperors had not forgotten that they once ruled the entire Roman Empire, and some of them attempted to reconquer the West. Justinian, who reigned from 527 to 565, was the last to try. Justinian was also the last Latin-speaking emperor in Constantinople. Greek language and social customs were so dominant in the Byzantine world that although the people of the empire still called themselves Romans, to westerners they were "the Greeks."

Emperor Justinian tried to unite the eastern and western parts of the sprawling Roman Empire. In this mosaic, he wears a diadem, a Byzantine-style crown, representing the shift in the Roman Empire to more eastern traditions.

In a private work called *The Secret History,* Justinian's official court historian, Procopius, recorded what he *really* thought of his emperor and patron. Procopius called Justinian "a moron" and wrote, "He was never truthful with anyone, but always guileful in what he said and did, yet easily hoodwinked by any who wanted to deceive him. His nature was an unnatural mix of folly and wickedness."

Justinian, who surrounded himself with dramatic people, married an intelligent, forceful woman whom some enemies considered a sorceress. Her name was Theodora, and she was very much her husband's partner in running the empire. Early in their reign, when rioters burned much of Constantinople and threatened to topple the couple from their thrones, Theodora refused to flee, declaring that she would rather die an empress than live in exile. She and Justinian managed to calm the riots and keep their thrones.

Justinian rebuilt Constantinople on a grand scale. The most monumental structure was a great domed church called Hagia Sophia (meaning "holy wisdom"), which still stands. One of the emperor's favorite ways to impress visiting barbarians was to take them to church at Hagia Sophia. The experience was overwhelming. In his *Secret History*, Procopius described its great dome as if it floated in the air, as if suspended by a chain from heaven. The church was lined with shimmering mosaics of gems and gold, and a row of windows around the base of the dome made the roof seem to float when seen from inside. Once the emperor had a child suspended from the ceiling to play the part of an angel, filling the dome with heavenly singing—although the child's thoughts about this perilous episode were not recorded.

Another of Justinian's achievements had far-reaching, long-lasting effects. By his time, Roman law was a jumble of old practices and imperial decrees. His legal scholars sifted through them, weeding out duplications and inconsisten-

A modern view of Hagia Sophia, the immense, lavishly decorated Christian church built under Justinian's rule in Constantinople (modern-day Istanbul). From the four slender towers, called minarets, criers call people to prayer in the Muslim tradition.

cies. They produced a unified code of laws, a summary of legal principles, and even a book for law students. Much later, in the 12th century, Justinian's collection of laws made its way to western Europe, where it shaped legal thinking and practice. Much modern commercial law, such as contracts, is rooted in the Roman law that Justinian preserved.

Also descended from Roman law were ideas about the relationship between rulers and their people—specifically the idea that emperors have to obey the law just as the people do, and that their power comes from the people. Justinian, however, tended to take law and government into his own hands, concentrating power in the office of the emperor. His subjects had little access to him, and those he did see had to lie on the floor in his presence.

When Justinian and Theodora tried to reconquer the western part of the old empire, they met with some success—at first. Their general destroyed the kingdom of the Vandals in North Africa and weakened the Ostrogoths, the Gothic people who had taken over Italy, by encouraging the Lombards to destroy their kingdom. In the end, though, Justinian held onto only the island of Sicily, some of southern Italy, and the Italian city of Ravenna, which the Byzantines controlled until the middle of the 8th century. Justinian had other problems, too. His campaigns and building projects had emptied the Byzantine treasury, and he faced war on the eastern border of his empire.

Justinian's enemy was the Persian Empire, based in what is now Iran. The Persians had threatened Byzantine security for a long time, going so far as to capture and enslave an earlier Byzantine emperor, and then kill and stuff him. Although the Byzantines defeated the Persians in 641, the long and draining series of wars left both empires weak.

CHARLEMAGNE REIGNS!

In western Europe, meanwhile, the Merovingians were also becoming weak. As their power dwindled, others waited in the wings to seize control of their kingdom. A family descended from bishops served the Merovingian kings as mayors of the palace. One of them, Charles Martel, was ruler in all but name. He was succeeded by his son, Pépin, who was not content to govern for the Merovingians—he wanted to be king in his own right. When a Lombard army threatened Rome, the pope asked Pépin for help. In reply, Pépin asked to become king. The pope answered that "the man who had the actual power was more deserving of the crown than one who was only a figurehead." Taking this as permission to overthrow the Merovingian monarch, Pépin declared himself king in 751, sending the former king off to a monastery. He then defeated the Lombards and gave the pope a large tract of land around Rome and Ravenna.

Pépin was known as Pépin the Short. With the help of the pope, he maneuvered his way to become king of the Franks and issued this silver coin with his name on it.

Pépin's two sons inherited his kingdom, but one died young. The other became one of the most important rulers of the Middle Ages: Carolus Magnus (Latin for Charles the Great), or Charlemagne. Charlemagne's biographer, Einhard, wrote, "Charles was large and strong... his height is well known to have been seven times the length of his foot... his eyes very large and animated, nose a little long, hair fair, and face laughing and merry." His dynasty is called Carolingian, a term that comes from his name. Charlemagne loved both Christianity and learning. While he ate, he had the books of Saint Augustine of Hippo read aloud to him. Einhard, described the king's belated efforts to learn to write: "He used to keep tablets and blanks in bed under his pillow, that at leisure hours he might accustom his hand to form the letters; however, as he did not begin his efforts in due season, but late in life, they met with ill success."

Charlemagne may not have learned to write, but he made certain that his children received an education, daughters as well as sons. He promoted education for others, too, starting schools in the cathedrals to educate the clergy and inviting scholars from northern England and other parts of Europe to live at his court. Charlemagne also took vigorous steps to spread Christianity. He didn't hesitate to use the threat of force—he told the Saxons of northern Germany that if they did not convert, he would put them all to death. They converted.

Charlemagne's military campaigns pushed the borders of the Franks' territory north into what is now the Netherlands, east across the Rhine River, and into other areas that even the Romans had not conquered. Then, after 32 years as king of the Franks, he received a letter asking for help. It came from Pope Leo III, whose enemies had removed him from office and cut out his tongue. Charlemagne took an army to Rome and reinstated the pope. Two days later, on Christmas Day, 800, the pope crowned Charlemagne

Charlemagne, sitting in a tent, is dressed for battle. His armed knights are either sleeping or already on horseback. Probably no name has echoed through the ages more than that of Charlemagne. A devout Christian and a great warrior, he also encouraged education, even though he could not read or write.

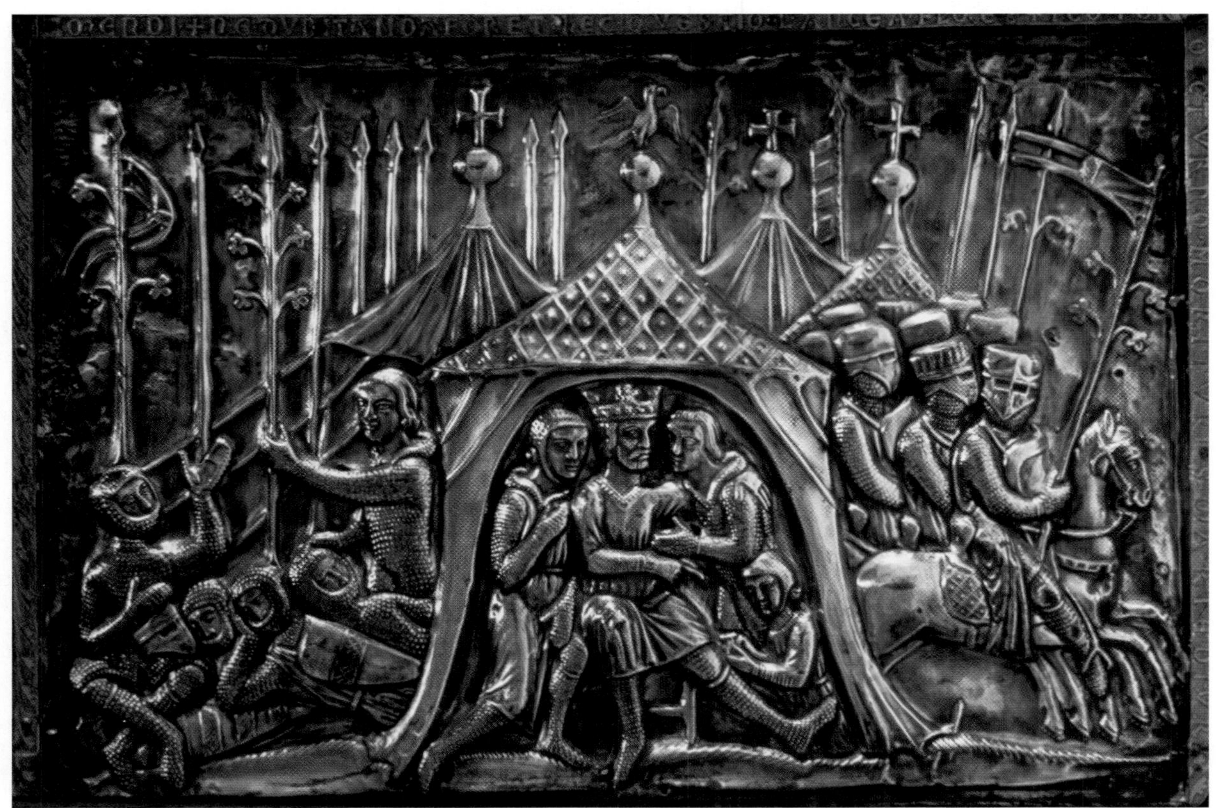

emperor. Although neither the pope nor Charlemagne had any legal rights over the imperial title in the West, Charlemagne's subjects acknowledged him as emperor.

The Carolingian Empire did not have much in common with the Byzantine Empire. The Byzantine emperors' incomes came from taxes on all their subjects, but Charlemagne's came from his own vast private estates. While the Byzantine rulers tended to hide themselves in their palaces, away from the public, Charlemagne spent much time traveling through his empire on horseback, accompanied by his household administrators. But even Charlemagne, with his great energy, could not govern his empire single-handed. He placed border regions, where newly conquered people often remained rebellious, under the control of leaders called marquises or dukes. In more settled areas, officials called counts handled administrative duties. Drawn from the Frankish upper class, these marquises, dukes, and counts were the beginning of a new European nobility.

At the other end of the Carolingian social scale were the agricultural peasants. Some were lifelong laborers on the old Roman estates. Others were nomadic tribespeople who had settled down to work the land for a living. Estate records from Charlemagne's time, which list the names and status of the peasants, reveal a mix of Roman and Germanic backgrounds.

One family had both biblical and Frankish names: a man named Abrahil was married to a woman named Berthildis, and their children were Abram (a biblical name) Avremarus, and Bertrada. The family's status was also mixed. Abrahil was a slave, which meant that he had to work for the owner of the estate and could not leave it. Berthildis was free, which meant that she owed labor on the estate in exchange for the use of the owner's land. But she could leave if she wanted to. Peasants seldom moved, however, because, like Berthildis, they were married to slaves.

Estates belonged to abbots, bishops, popes, nobles, kings, and emperors. On an estate, the best agricultural land was set aside for the owner's use. The rest was divided

"For to light candles before rocks and trees and streams and at crossroads—is this anything else but the worship of the devil? To observe divinations and auguries and days of the idols—is this anything else but the worship of the devil?"

—Bishop Martin of Braga, condemning the superstitions, traditional practices, and remnants of belief in the old gods that survived in the Carolingian empire, Spain, 6th century

among the peasants, who grew crops and raised livestock to feed their families. They paid the owner for the use of the land in labor, goods, or rent money. Abrahil shared his farm with two other men. All were tenants of the lord who owned the land. In return for the use of the land, they carted the lord's goods to market, carried his firewood in the winter, mended his fences, plowed his fields, harvested his crops, and paid the lord four pennies a year in tax.

For Abrahil's family, a typical spring day was hard work from dawn to dusk. Berthildis rose early to light the fire in the family's hut and heat the morning meal of cooked grain. Abrahil took his ox to the lord's fields where, overseen by the lord's stewards, or managers, he and the other men of the village did the plowing. Young Abram helped his father by prodding the ox. Eight-year-old Avremarus fetched water from the well and then took the cow to pasture. In the hut, Berthildis placed the baby Bertrada in a cradle near the warm fire and then heated water for brewing beer. Returning tired in the evening, Abrahil, Abram, and Avremarus ate bread and peas boiled with ham and drank beer before falling asleep on straw pallets, covered by rough linen sheets and woolen blankets woven by Berthildis.

The next day, and the day after that, would be much the same. Other than the different tasks that came with changing seasons, peasants' lives held little variety except for feast days—religious holidays scattered through the year. A visit

Medieval peasants produced crops and raised animals for their own families and also worked for the lord of the manor. Among their many daily activities, women carried water, milked the cows, and cared for the sheep. The illustration is from a 14th-century manuscript.

from an official might break the monotony. Charlemagne himself might pass by with his group of attendants, including an elephant that had been a gift from far-off Persia. If Abrahil and Berthildis witnessed such an event, they would talk about it for years.

After Charlemagne died in 814, his empire fell into disorder. His son Louis, who inherited the empire, was neither a good statesman nor a skilled military leader. Louis divided the empire among his three sons and gave them some responsibility for ruling, but they had no sooner claimed their lands and titles than they started fighting among themselves, just like the Frankish princes of old. In 843, three years after Louis's death, the three signed the Treaty of Verdun, dividing Charlemagne's empire into three parts: France, Germany, and the "middle kingdom," which ran from northern Italy into the Netherlands. That middle kingdom was destined to be a source of conflict. For centuries, France and Germany would claim parts of it as their own. Some historians even claim that World Wars I and II in the 20th century were the direct result of the Treaty of Verdun.

Compared with his ineffective descendants, Charlemagne was remembered as an extraordinary leader. Not all his

Omens Foretell an Emperor's Death

EINHARD, LIFE OF CHARLEMAGNE, AROUND 829–836

Medieval Europeans often interpreted natural events and disasters as omens, signs foretelling a major event. Of course, people usually remembered these signs after *the event had taken place. Such was the case following the death of Charlemagne on January 28, 814. Einhard, one of the emperor's biographers, spent the early part of his life in Charlemagne's court and knew the emperor well. He was a member of the clergy and wrote his biography at the request of Charlemagne's son, Louis the Pious, between 820 and 830.*

Very many omens had portended [Charlemagne's] approaching end, a fact that he had recognized as well as others. Eclipses both of the sun and moon were very frequent during the last three years of his life, and a black spot was visible on the sun for the space of seven days. The gallery between the basilica [church building] and the palace, which he had built at great pains and labor, fell in sudden ruin to the ground on the day of the Ascension of our Lord. The wooden bridge over the Rhine at Mayence, which he had caused to be constructed with admirable skill, at the cost of ten years' hard work, so that it seemed as if it might last forever, was so completely consumed in three hours by an accidental fire that not a single splinter of it was left, except what was under water.

Moreover, one day in his last campaign into Saxony against Godfred, King of the Danes, [Charlemagne] himself saw a ball of fire fall suddenly from the heavens with great light, just as he was leaving camp before sunrise to set out on the march. It rushed across the clear sky from right to left, and everybody was wondering what was the meaning of the sign, when the horse which he was riding gave a sudden plunge, head foremost, and fell, and threw him to the ground so heavily that his cloak buckle was broken and his sword belt shattered. . . . He happened to have a javelin in his hand when he was thrown, and this was struck from his grasp with such force that it was found lying at a distance of twenty feet or more from the spot.

Einhard (left) writes about the life of Charlemagne, while the emperor (right) leads his troops into battle.

campaigns, however, had ended in victory. In the 770s he had hoped to conquer Spain, but his plan was halted by another force—a force set in motion years earlier by the visions of an Arabian prophet.

MUHAMMAD AND A NEW FAITH

Arabia was never part of the Roman Empire, but its merchants traded with the Byzantines as well as Persians. The Arabs lived in family and tribal units. They worshipped many gods. The city of Mecca was a religious center because it had a shrine called the Ka'ba, which housed symbols of the Arabs' gods. In this city a man named Muhammad was born around 571. Working as a caravan trader for a wealthy woman who later became his wife, Muhammad met Jews and Christians in towns on the edge of Byzantine territory.

In his late 30s, after he received mystical revelations that he attributed to God, he began preaching a new faith. Like the Jewish and Christian religions, it was based on the worship of a single God. At first Muhammad converted only his wife and a few relatives, but the merchants of Mecca became worried, fearing that he was discrediting the Ka'ba.

To escape the merchants' wrath, Muhammad fled to a city later known as Medina, where he preached and gathered followers. Their notes on his sermons formed the basis of the Quran, the holy book of Islam, the religion Muhammad founded. In 630, Muhammad and his followers returned in triumph to Mecca. He spent his final two years unifying the Arabs under Islam, creating a state in which he was both religious and political leader. Muhammad regarded himself as the last in a series of prophets that included Moses and Jesus. He told his followers to submit to the will of Allah, the single, almighty God. The basic tenet of Islam was, "There is no god but Allah, and Muhammad is his prophet." Those who followed Islam were assured of salvation.

After Muhammad's death, a series of his followers ruled the state he had founded. These *khailifa,* or caliphs—from the Arabic word for "successor"—guided the rapid spread of Islam. In the first wave of conquest, from 632 to 655,

Arab armies conquered Syria, Egypt, and the Persian Empire. The conquered populations found Islam attractive, and many Christians, Jews, and Persians converted.

The Arabs proved remarkably adaptable to new circumstances. Upon reaching the Mediterranean Sea, for example, they became excellent sailors, crossing the sea to conquer Sicily and other Byzantine territories. They borrowed from—and sometimes improved on—the art, architecture, and intellectual achievements of those they conquered.

During the Abbasid dynasty, from the 9th to the 13th century, descendants of Abbas, uncle of Muhammad, held the caliphate. Persian scholars gathered to discuss their work in palaces and mosques. Great advances were made in mathematics, astronomy, medicine, and literature.

After taking Baghdad, the capital of the Persian Empire, which included Iran and Iraq, the Arabs mastered the Persians' knowledge of astronomy. They also discovered the works of the ancient Greek philosophers and medical experts in manuscripts that had reached Persia by a curious path. Long before, when Christianity became the dominant religion in the Roman Empire, intellectuals who remained true to the old gods left the Christian world and settled in Persia, taking their books with them. By the time of the Islamic conquest, these works had been translated into Persian. Arab scholars translated them into Arabic, adding their own commentaries.

Muhammad's faith still spread widely after his death. Arab armies stripped territory from the Byzantine Empire, leaving it with only Constantinople, the Balkan Peninsula, and a portion of Asia Minor, or Turkey. Even in this shrunken form, the Byzantine Empire was a wealthy and powerful force in the eastern Mediterranean. Constantinople, with a million inhabitants, was one of the great early medieval cities; other Byzantine cities produced silks, glass, tapestries, ivory carvings, and fine jewelry that were much prized in the West.

The Arabs also moved into North Africa, where they destroyed the remnants of Byzantine rule. They crossed the Mediterranean into Spain and overthrew the Visigoths. The Moors—a term used by European Christians for the Muslims who had come to Spain by way of Morocco in North Africa—might have gone on to conquer all Europe. But after they crossed the Pyrenees Mountains into southwestern France, they ran into an army commanded by Charlemagne's grandfather, Charles Martel, the mighty mayor of the Merovingian palace, who earned the nickname "Hammer of Christendom" for turning back the Islamic invaders in 732.

Spain, however, remained under Arab control for centuries. It was one of many caliphates, subdivisions ruled by a caliph that formed when the Arabian Empire split along political and religious lines. The main religious split, which endures today, was between the Sunnis and the Shiites. The

Shiites were followers of Muhammad's son-in-law, Ali, and argued that only his descendants could rule. The Sunnis accepted another line of caliphs, but also accepted the *Sunnas,* traditions not included in the *Quran.* Yet despite political and religious divisions, the Arabic language and a shared intellectual and social heritage united the Islamic world.

Of the Byzantine, Frankish, and Muslim empires, the Muslim one had the greatest scholarship. Muslim scholars studied Greek philosophy and science from the West, and Indian mathematics and Persian astronomy from the East. In the 8th century, they introduced the Indian idea of zero and nine digits to the West, so that the system came to be known as Arabic numerals (though it would take the Europeans another half century to adopt the system and write, for example, 1276 instead of MCCLXXVI). Throughout the Middle Ages, Muslim scholars not only preserved the learning of the ancient world, they added to it. They improved the astrolabe, a tool the Greeks had invented to navigate, and expanded on Greek medical knowledge. In Islamic cities in Spain, Sicily, and southern Italy, Jews translated Islamic texts from Arabic into their own Hebrew language. Later, Christian scholars translated the Hebrew texts into Latin, bringing a wealth of knowledge to Christian Europe.

Medieval camel drivers used an instrument called an astrolabe to fix their position in the desert by plotting the positions of stars in the night sky. Europeans copied the idea from the Muslims and used astrolabes to navigate at sea.

CHAPTER 4

A GOOD KNIGHT'S WORK

WAR AND FEUDALISM

One day in the mid-9th century in England, a boy named Alfred sat with his mother and brothers, looking at a book. It was a volume of poetry from their people, the Saxons, who were Germanic but had lived in England for several centuries. Alfred's mother told the boys that she would give the book to the first one who learned it by heart. The book was beautiful, with large, colorfully painted capital letters, and Alfred yearned to possess it. He took it to his tutor, who read it aloud just once. Alfred then returned to his mother and repeated the poems exactly. She kept her word and gave him the book. But Alfred was more than a book-loving medieval youth with an excellent memory. He was heir to the throne of Wessex, a kingdom in southwestern England. Alfred would become renowned in his time and afterward for saving part of England from fierce, terrifying enemies who swept over Europe like a tidal wave.

This wooden warrior's head from around 850 decorated a wagon found in a Viking grave. Vikings often buried their dead with objects that they thought would be useful in the afterlife.

Those enemies were the Vikings, men from the fjords of Scandinavia. Their native region had little agricultural land, and by the late 8th century the population had outgrown the land's ability to support it. The Scandinavian peoples—Swedes, Danes, and Norwegians—turned to fishing, trade, and plunder. They developed boats that could navigate both the rough Atlantic Ocean and the shallow rivers of Europe. Carrying crews of 40 to 100 men, driven by oars and sails, these craft carried the Swedes across the Baltic Sea and down rivers to the Black Sea and Constantinople. Along the way, Swedish Vikings founded the cities of Novgorod and Kiev in modern-day Russia and the Ukraine. Known as the Rus, these Vikings gave their name to Russia.

The Danes and Norwegians came to Europe as traders but later turned to raiding. They plundered monasteries, towns, and villages, taking gold and silver and livestock. They killed those who resisted them and destroyed valuable manuscripts. The feeble governments of 9th-century Europe were no match for them. Ireland had never had a strong government, England was split into small kingdoms, and weak kings ruled the divided Carolingian Empire. Who could withstand the determined pirates from Scandinavia?

England, wealthy and close at hand, was their first target. In 787, Vikings destroyed the monasteries of northern England. Then they attacked and plundered London on the Thames River, but they could not get farther inland because London's bridge was too low for them to go under. With typical vigor, the Vikings solved that problem: They attached ropes from their boats to pilings driven into the riverbed, then rowed rapidly downstream, tearing down the bridge.

By the mid-9th century, Viking raiders had taken Ireland. An Irish monk wrote of the Viking raids,

> [A] hundred hard-steeled iron heads on one neck, and a hundred sharp, ready, cool, never rusting, brazen tongues in each head, and a hundred garrulous, loud, unceasing voices from each tongue . . . could not recount . . . what all . . . suffered . . . of hardship, of injury, and of oppression, in every house, from these valiant, wrathful, foreign, purely pagan people.

"Yet amid the wars and many hindrances of this present life, and amid the assaults of the pagans, and his daily illness, the king ceased not from the governance of the kingdom and. . . . the reading of books in the Saxon tongue."

—Asser, Alfred's biographer, from his account of the king's life, 893

Very wealthy Vikings were buried in their boats. This large ship was excavated in 1904 in Oslo, Norway. Bodies were also buried with horses, dogs, beds, and many other items that the person had used in life.

The Vikings also ventured up the rivers leading into France. They reached Paris in 845 and Aachen, Charlemagne's former capital, in 881, before going into Spain and the Mediterranean Sea. Vikings sailed westward as well. Venturing far into the North Atlantic, they settled Iceland and Greenland in the late 9th century.

In the 400s, Germanic invaders began to arrive in Britain. By 800, one of these new ruling tribes, the Angles, had given the land a new name: England.

SWAT! VIKINGS DEFEAT CHARLES THE FAT

A few European rulers managed to halt the Vikings. Alfred of Wessex stopped their advance in the 870s and even won back some English territory from them. He established a

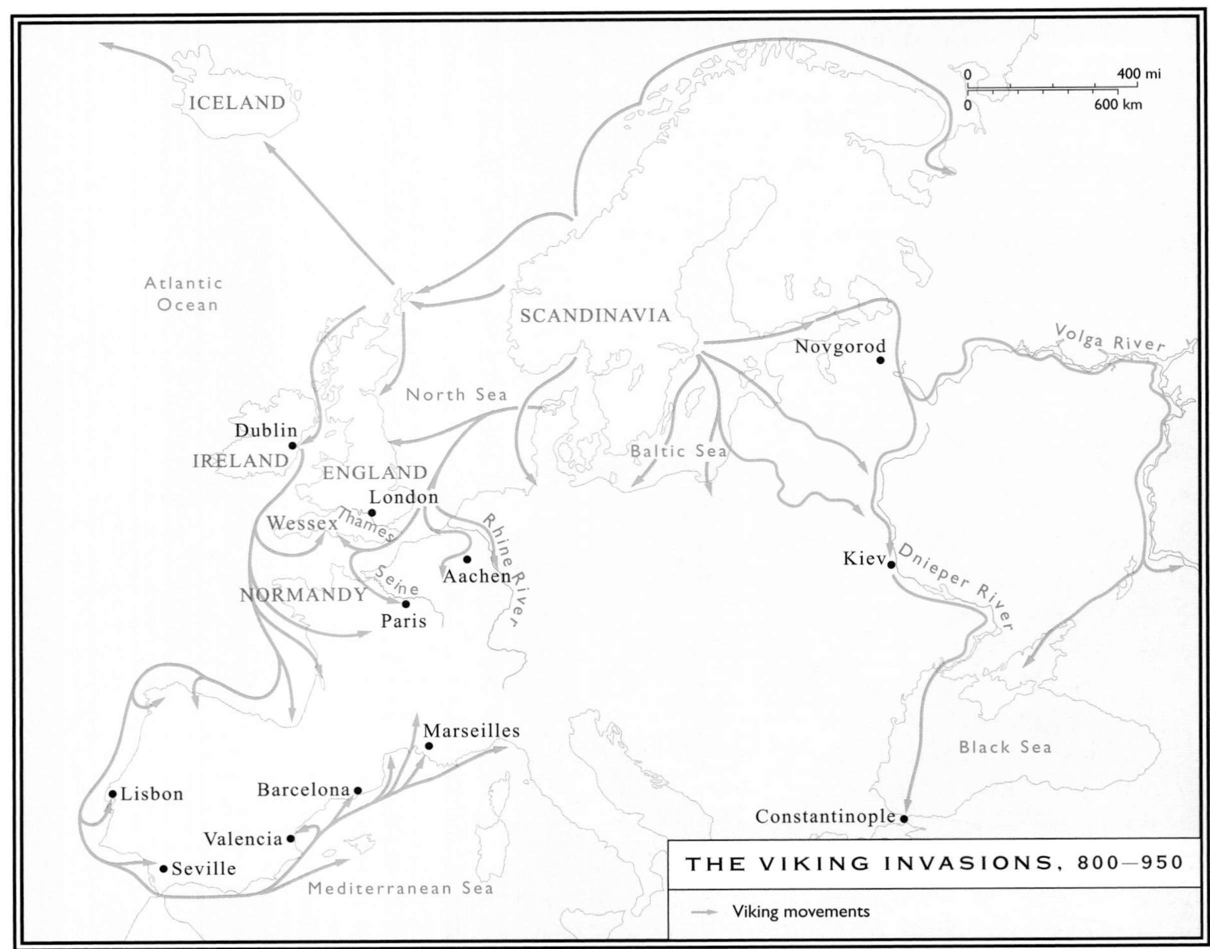

diagonal boundary across England, leaving the north to the Vikings and protecting the south. To this day, places in the territory north of this boundary have Danish names. In the German-speaking eastern part of the former Carolingian Empire, the king not only defeated the Danes but also fought off another group of invaders, the Magyars, or Hungarians. Traveling on horseback, the Hungarian raiders took plunder and murdered the people. They eventually settled in what is today called Hungary.

In the weaker western part of the Carolingian Empire, the Vikings gained control of a region on the Atlantic coast of France. The Carolingian king granted their leader the title of duke. The territory they controlled was a dukedom called Normandy after the Norse who settled it (this name for Scandinavians refers to the north from which they came). They wanted to plunder eastern France by taking their boats up the Seine River, but the bridges of Paris were not easy to destroy, and the count of Paris had strung a chain across the river. The Vikings offered to spare Paris if the people would let them pass. The Parisians refused, and the city withstood two years of siege. In the end, a Carolingian king named Charles the Fat permitted them to plunder beyond Paris.

The Alfred Jewel was discovered near Athelney, in the south of England, where King Alfred had founded a monastery. Its use is unknown, though the king probably gave it as a gift to a bishop or some other official. The words in Old English "Alfred ordered me to be made" are carved in the gold band.

When the kings of France failed to protect their people from the Vikings, the people sought help from local strongmen. A nobleman named Odo became king in 888 after successfully defending Paris from the Vikings. His nephew Hugh Capet, the count of Paris, became king in 987. Hugh's successors, the Capetian dynasty, ruled France until the early 14th century. At first, though, Hugh ruled only the area around Paris. The rest of France was under the control of powerful nobles.

Nobles maintained households of armed servants to help them defend their territory. All noblemen trained to become knights, or warriors. A knight took an oath of loyalty, or fealty, by kneeling before his lord and placing his hands in the lord's hands, promising to protect him. A medieval law book provided a model for the wording of the

Count Roland's Last Stand

AN ANONYMOUS FRENCHMAN, THE SONG OF ROLAND, MID-11TH CENTURY

Both Vikings and Europeans of the early feudal period enjoyed poems about battles, tales of deceit and valor, and deeds of gods, kings, and adventurers. The Song of Roland *tells the story of the heroic last stand of Count Roland, vassal of Charles, and his friend, Oliver. Roland is too proud to call Charlemagne to the rescue by blowing the Oliphant, a horn made from a carved elephant tusk. In the poem, Charlemagne is an old and respected king who is presented as the ideal feudal ruler. The text refers to Muslims as pagans, showing how little the Franks understood Islam.*

Roland's a hero, and Oliver is wise;
Both are so brave men marvel at their deeds.
When they mount chargers, take up their swords and shields,
No death itself could drive them from the field.
They are good men; their words are fierce and proud.
With wrathful speed the pagans ride to war.
Oliver says, "Roland, you see them now.
They're very close, the king too far away.
You were too proud to sound the Oliphant:
If Charles were with us, we would not come to grief.
Look up above us, close to the Gate of Spain:
There stands the guard—who would not pity them!
To fight this battle means not to fight again."
Roland replies, "Don't speak so foolishly!
Cursed be the heart that cowers in the breast!
We'll hold our ground; if they will meet us here,
Our foes will find us ready with sword and spear."
. . . At Roncevaux Count Roland passes by,
Riding his charger, swift-running Veillantif.
He's armed for battle, splendid in shining [chain] mail.
As he parades, he brandishes his lance,
Turning the point straight up against the sky,
And from the spearhead a banner flies, pure white,
With long gold fringes that beat against his hands.
Fair to behold, he laughs, serene and gay.
Now close behind him comes Oliver, his friend,
With all the Frenchmen cheering their mighty lord.
Fiercely his eyes confront the Saracens [Muslim residents of Spain];
Humbly and gently he gazes at the Franks,
Speaking to them with gallant courtesy:
"Barons, my lords, softly now, keep the pace!
Here come the pagans looking for martyrdom.
We'll have such plunder before the day is out,
As no French king has ever won before!"
And at this moment the armies join in war.

oath: "Hear this, lord, that I will bear you fealty in life and limb, in body, goods, and earthly honor, so help me God." Some remained warriors all their lives. Others became lords, with lands and titles that they took for themselves or were given by higher lords. Medieval society was organized into many layers, with each layer dominating those beneath it. The king was at the top, followed by the nobles, which included dukes, counts, marquises, and barons. Popes, bishops, and abbots were usually sons of nobles and were members of the ruling elite. In the 12th century the titles, power, and relations among these elites became more fixed.

22 OXEN WILL BUY YOU A KNIGHT

A knight's training was long and expensive. Noble boys began preparing for knighthood when they were seven or eight. They learned to ride horses, wear helmets and armor, and use swords and spears. Warfare changed in the 12th century. The Romans had used foot soldiers, and the Germanic tribes had used highly mobile horsemen. But as

The Carolingians waged war using large horses that could support a heavily armed rider. Stirrups, such as those shown on this vase from the late 12th century, helped knights to stay in their saddles even when hit by the lance of a mounted enemy charging toward them at full speed.

armor and weapons became heavier, knights began using larger war horses that could carry armored fighters bearing shields, lances, and swords. The cost of a knight's armor and weapons was the same as the price for 22 oxen. A peasant's largest plow team was eight oxen—so becoming a knight was far beyond any peasant's means.

Another military development was the defensive fortress, or castle. The earliest defenses were known as motte-and-bailey castles. The motte was a natural hill or one that had been built up from nearby stone and earth, topped with a wooden fort or tower (in time the wooden walls gave way to stone). The bailey was an area enclosed by a low wall, which either surrounded the motte or was next to it. The bailey was big enough to hold the animals and other valuables of the lord and his peasants. If raiders took the bailey, the people could retreat into the motte fort—and, they hoped, at least save their lives.

Castles were an investment of labor and money. The people who built them became the protectors of their neighbors, but the neighbors had to repay the favor. If the neighbors were warriors, they had to fight for the castle owner in exchange for his protection. If they were peasants, they had to work his land. Modern historians use the term feudalism for this network of personal ties and mutual obligations, which held together medieval society and government.

Powerful lords needed fighters to protect and administer their territory, so they offered land to less powerful warriors, who then became their vassals, from the Latin word *vassus,* meaning servant. In return, vassals promised to look after their lords' interests. The grant of land was called a fief (rhymes with "leaf"), which comes from the old German word *fihu* meaning property. In theory, the king owned all the land; dukes and counts simply used it at his pleasure. They, in turn, granted it to the barons and knights. But because the kings were weak, dukes and counts had considerable control over their lands. Bishops and abbots also had fiefs and granted parcels of land to vassals.

Feudalism, which originated in France and spread to Germany and England, imposed duties and granted rights.

A vassal who received a fief swore to be loyal and serve his lord in times of need. In the early 12th century, for example, a vassal swore his loyalty to Count William of Flanders, modern-day Belgium, with these words: "I promise on my faith that I will in future be faithful to Count William and will observe my homage to him completely against all persons in good faith and without deceit." Fighting was a vassal's first obligation. The vassal had to serve his lord in war at his own expense, providing armor, horses, and men, but, if a period of service lasted longer than 40 days, the lord helped pay the cost. The vassal also had to accompany his lord in times of peace, be present at the lord's castle for two or three months each year, and contribute to the lord's expenses.

Lords reserved the right to reclaim land from rebellious vassals. In practice, however, reclaiming land could be difficult, because an angry vassal might attack the lord's castle or cause a revolt among his fellow vassals. A more convenient solution was to control inheritance. When a vassal died, the lord had the right to relief, which meant imposing a tax for passing the estate to the vassal's heir. If a vassal died leaving children under the age of 21, the lord claimed the children as his wards until they reached that age. During this period, the lord took the income from their estate. He also

Arundel Castle in Sussex, England, began as a fortress on a hill known as a motte-and-bailey castle, around 1068. A stone stairway leads up the motte, or hill, to the site where the original bailey, or enclosure, once stood.

had the right to marry the vassal's widow and daughters to anyone he chose.

Solemn oaths of loyalty from vassals and promises of protection from lords in the 12th century created more order than had been known in the two previous two centuries. Still, small battles over land were frequent in feudal Europe. Conflicts arose when vassals accepted fiefs from more than one lord and wound up with competing loyalties. Other fights broke out when someone inherited a fief but could not defend it. On such occasions, rival nobles fought over the land on the battlefield or asked their lords to intervene.

The laws of inheritance produced a body of restless fighting men. The Frankish custom of dividing estates equally among all sons had given way to primogeniture, or inheritance by the firstborn son. (If there were no sons, daughters inherited in equal portions.) Without land, younger sons needed other ways to make a living. Some became priests or monks—occasionally against their wills. But many younger sons who had been raised to be knights were unsuited to the religious life. Some became lords' vassals and earned a fief this way, while others tried to conquer land for themselves.

In this time of conflict over land, noblewomen had to be able to control their castles when their husbands or fathers were away fighting. Although they were not trained to fight, these resourceful women learned to administer estates, run households full of rough warriors, and organize the defense of a besieged castle. A woman who inherited a fief took the same vows of loyalty to the lord that a man would take; she also had to supply a knight to fight in her place. The same was true of abbots and bishops who held fiefs.

Noble marriages were not made for love but to create alliances between families. A noblewoman who had no brothers was a valuable heiress because her husband would get the use of her fief. Such women were married off by their fathers or lords when they were quite young. A girl or woman had no say in the matter—she would simply be married to the man with the best potential for political

Medieval farmers adopted the horse collar, which distributed the weight of the load around a horse's shoulders so it could pull a plow. Improved plow technology, as shown in this 15th-century illustration, revolutionized farming in the Middle Ages.

alliance, land gain, or military aid. Membership in the ranks of nobles was hereditary, which meant that the privileges of nobility could be gained only by birth. The noble class and the clergy, many of whom were younger sons of nobles, made up about 5 to 10 percent of the total population. The other 90 to 95 percent were peasants. Artisans and merchants were few, for agriculture was medieval Europe's main economic activity.

Three men work together to sharpen a knife: two turn the handles that move the grindstone up and down while a third (center) carefully presses a knife blade against the surface of the moving stone.

THE VILLEIN OF THE STORY

Peasant life had also changed since the time of Charlemagne. The adoption of the horse collar, which distributed weight around a horse's shoulders rather than pulling a strap against its neck, let horses pull heavily loaded carts. The horseshoe also came into use, keeping horses' hooves from splitting when the horses hauled heavy loads. Improved plows, with blades to cut heavy sod, meant that previously unfarmed lands could now be brought into cultivation. These improvements in agriculture helped peasants produce much more food than before.

Agriculture, by the 12th century, was organized around long parcels of land called manors, which usually included a village. A fief could be as small as part of a manor or as large as many manors. Within each manor, peasants lived in village houses amid gardens and outbuildings. The village had a church and priest's residence. It might also have a manor house, where the lord stayed when he visited, and a residence for his estate manager, the steward. Around the village were the fields. Each field was several hundred acres in area and was divided into strips. The best strips were the lord's. Others were reserved for the local priest. The rest were divided among the peasants. Each family received a mix of good and bad farmland, but families' total acreage varied from five or six acres for the poorer families to thirty or more for the most prosperous.

Each peasant's duties were spelled out in the *custumal*, the register of customary services and rents that each family owed. Peasants could be free or unfree. Some peasants descended from slaves, some lost their freedom by conquest or debt, and some kept ownership of their land. The unfree peasants were called serfs or villeins (old French for "village dwellers"). On the surface, the differences between the two groups were small. Both had to work for the lord. Serfs, though, bore additional burdens. While free peasants owned their lands, serfs only had the right to rent their fathers' land—and to do so, they had to pay death dues to the lord. The dues usually included a serf's best plow oxen as well as a fee. Serfs also paid annual rent. And while free peasants could leave the manor as they wished, serfs had to pay the lord if they wished to leave. A serf also owed special rents and gifts to the lord, including fowl on feast days such as Christmas, and eggs at Easter; the modern customs of eating goose or chicken for Christmas dinner and decorating eggs for Easter come from these practices.

Marriages between free and unfree peasants were so common that the division between the two groups grew

"Electeus a slave and his wife a colona, [peasant] by the name of Landina. . . . they live in Neuillay. He holds half a farm. . . . He plows in the winter field and in the spring field. He carts manure to the lord's field."

—Capitulary *De Villis, Instructions for a Village*, 806–829 blurred. A free peasant could move his family if he wished, but there were few places to go. If he had land and a lord who shielded him from raiding armies, he was happy enough to stay where he was. Livelihoods were so chancy that people were grateful to have land to work and protection during invasions and local skirmishes.

Two centuries after King Alfred ruled Wessex, medieval society was changing, in England and across Europe. On the European continent, feudal society had become more organized and formal. Viking raiders settled down and became Christian; they no longer roamed the seas. Peasants could till the soil with less fear of raids. But the desire of nobles for more land led to further conquests. A weak king ruled England, lands to the east of Germany were sparsely settled, and Christians began to look at conquest in Spain.

This cross, a Christian symbol of the martyred Jesus, has been carved with Jesus dressed in Viking tradition. By the 11th century the Vikings had blended with the European people they had invaded.

CHAPTER 5

BATTLE AND BARTER

FROM THE NORMAN CONQUEST TO THE RISE OF TRADE

Because of his religious habits, King Edward, who ruled England in the mid-11th century, was called the Confessor. He was a descendant of Alfred, the king of Wessex who had repelled the Viking invasion two centuries earlier. Since Alfred's day, the Vikings had settled down—but other foreign powers still longed to rule England. Edward's death gave them their chance.

King Edward's wife was Edith, the sister of an Anglo-Saxon nobleman named Harold Godwinson. Edith, however, bore no children—and therefore Edward had no heir. As he aged, three powerful men dreamed of inheriting his kingdom. One was Harold Godwinson, who claimed that his sister's marriage entitled him to the throne. Although Harold was not of royal blood, the Anglo-Saxon people of England supported his claim. In Norway, King Harald Hardrada also claimed the right to the English throne because he was related to a Danish king who had once ruled England. The third contender was Duke William of Normandy, the region in France that had been settled by Vikings. King Edward was half Norman and had grown up in Normandy, and William argued that Edward had promised him the throne. Each of the three, determined to take control of England as soon as Edward the Confessor died, disputed the others' claims.

In 1066, as the king lay on his deathbed, a comet appeared in the sky. Modern astronomers know that it was Halley's Comet, but the people of medieval England saw it as a sign of terrible events to come. They were right.

When Edward died, the Anglo-Saxons chose Harold Godwinson as their new king. Harald Hardrada of Norway immediately invaded northern England and advanced on the city of York. Harold Godwinson managed to defeat his

Norwegian foe, but two weeks later, William's Norman fleet landed in southern England. William was well prepared with supplies, warhorses, and even a prefabricated castle. His army included many of the younger sons of the Norman and French nobility, ambitious to win fiefs of their own.

The two armies met at Hastings, a town on the southern coast of England. Harold's troops were situated on a rise, and made a wall to protect themselves. The Normans, at a disadvantage, had to attack going uphill. At some point, however, the wall broke down, and Harold was shot in the eye with an arrow. The Normans were victorious.

One victory was not a conquest, as Duke William knew. He headed west with his army, building castles along the way. Turning north, he fought his way across the countryside to London, his final target. Once he controlled the city, he built his biggest castle, the Tower of London, which still

The Normans had this wall hanging—called the Bayeux tapestry for the town in France where it hangs—made to tell their side of the events leading up to their victory in the Battle of Hastings. In this scene, Harold's fleet crosses the English Channel. The tapestry is really embroidered, or sewn, rather than woven like a rug.

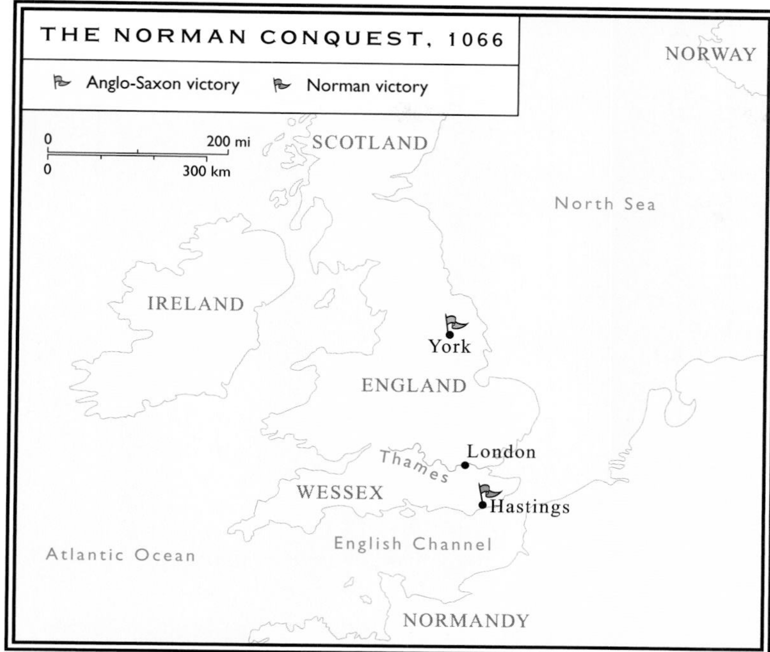

stands today. All along the route of his conquest, William killed or drove off the Anglo-Saxon noblemen, giving their land to his followers. He also married the widows and daughters of the Anglo-Saxons to his followers. In this way, the Normans brought the feudal system to England. The English peasants, formerly free, became serfs living on manors run by the Norman overlords. And Duke William became known to history as William the Conqueror. William of Malmesbury, a monk born to an English mother and a Norman father about 20 years after the Norman Conquest, wrote in his history, "This [Battle of Hastings] was a fatal day to England, a melancholy havoc of our dear country, through its change of masters."

The Norman Conquest of England was, in a way, the last of the Scandinavian invasions. For several hundred years, pressure from northern warriors and their descendants had shaped the history of England and France. In Germany, things had gone somewhat differently. The German lands had suffered fewer and milder Viking attacks. German rulers, however, had had to deal with other problems.

The Conquered and Their Conqueror

ENGLISH MONKS, THE ANGLO-SAXON CHRONICLE, AROUND 874–1187

To see the Norman Conquest through English eyes, historians turn to the Anglo-Saxon Chronicle, *a record of early-medieval English history. It had been started by monks at various monasteries in the days of King Alfred and continued through the death of William the Conqueror in 1187. The* Chronicle *describes the common folks' opinion of William. While complaining that William was greedy and that he denied the people of their rights to hunt, the historians do say that William was "a very wise and great man, and more honored and more powerful than any of his predecessors."*

He had castles built
And poor men hard oppressed.
The king was so very stark [harsh]
And deprived his underlings of many a mark
Of gold and more hundreds of pounds of silver,
That he took by weight and with great injustice
From his people with little need for such a
deed.
Into avarice did he fall
And loved greediness above all.
He made great protection for the game
And imposed laws for the same,
That who so slew hart or hind [male and
female deer]
Should be made blind.

He preserved the harts and boars
And loved the stags as much
As if he were their father.
Moreover, for the hares did he decree that
they should go free.
Powerful men complained of it and poor men
lamented it,
But so fierce was he that he cared not for the
rancor of them all,
But they had to follow out the king's will
entirely
If they wished to live or hold their land,
Property or estate, or his favor great.
Alas! woe, that any man so proud should go,
And exalt himself and reckon himself above
all men!
May Almighty God show mercy to his soul
And grant unto him forgiveness for his sins.

Monks chronicled the events leading to William the Conqueror's victory in the Battle of Hastings. The initial letter in this 12th-century manuscript is elaborately decorated with a miniature illustration showing William on a throne.

GREGORY WINS POPULAR VOTE

In the mid-10th century, King Otto I the Great managed to bring some unity to Germany and even to the "middle kingdom" carved out in the Treaty of Verdun a century earlier. Otto defeated the Hungarians and Slavs in eastern Europe and began to convert these peoples to Christianity. He also marched into Italy to rescue the pope from local nobility, much as Charlemagne had done. In 962 he followed in Charlemagne's footsteps by taking the title Roman Emperor.

Emperors or not, Otto and his successors found it no easy task to rule the Germans. The vassals of feudal Germany were very powerful; they kept the right to elect and dethrone their kings. To take some power away from the

Saint Maurice brings Otto I into the presence of Christ. Otto carries a replica of the church he has built in honor of Saint Maurice. Saint Peter stands to the right holding his traditional symbol, two keys. The followers of Otto were great patrons of the church.

"Irene [to her persecutor]: From this [martyrdom] comes a deed of greatest joy for me, but for you of greatest sorrow. For the cruelty of your wickedness, you shall be condemned to hell."

—Roswitha of Gandersheim, recounts in her play *Dulcitius* the martyrdom of three maidens, 10th century

vassals, the emperors began appointing bishops and abbots to govern their territory. Not only were these educated men good administrators, but they were also loyal to the emperor who appointed them.

Learning flourished in Germany, encouraged by Otto and later emperors. One outstanding German scholar of the 10th century was the nun Roswitha of Gandersheim. The daughter of a noble family in the Duchy of Saxony, she was put at an early age into a Benedictine nunnery where she received a good education. Early in her studies, she wrote religious poetry about the miracles of the Virgin Mary. She then read the comedies of ancient Roman playwrights and was charmed by their language. Realizing that plays could be used to teach religion, Roswitha began writing dramas—the first plays written since Roman times. They dealt with religious subjects, such as the martyrdom of a young Christian woman in the Roman Empire. Finally, Roswitha wrote histories, including the *The Deeds of Otto,* which records the reign of Otto I the Great.

The other great scholar of the age had a very different life and career. Gerbert of Aurillac in France came from a peasant family, but local monks recognized his genius and educated him. He went to Spain, where he lived among Arab and Hebrew scholars in Barcelona. Although he studied with Christian scholars there because he did not know Arabic, he learned about Arab mathematics and astronomy. He knew so much that after he died a rumor started that he was actually an evil magician. In reality, he was a man ahead of his time. For example, he tried to convince Europeans to give up Roman numerals in favor of the far simpler Arabic digits. Gerbert's fame brought him the support of the German emperor, who made him pope. The peasant boy ended his career as Pope Sylvester II.

During the lifetimes of Roswitha and Gerbert, religious feeling gained strength across Europe. In 910 the duke of Aquitaine, a large province in France, founded a monastery at Cluny, France. Its abbot, however, was answerable only to the pope, not to the duke. As the monastery gained respect, other monasteries that had strayed from the Benedictine rule reformed their practices. Once lay people, or ordinary citizens, stopped being afraid that their churches would be destroyed in warfare, they began contributing to the building

This church in Toulouse, southern France, called Saint-Sernin, is a Romanesque masterpiece. Buildings in the Romanesque style tended to be low and their walls were thick because a huge amount of masonry was needed to hold up the stone ceilings. Windows were small with rounded arches.

of parish churches, cathedrals, and new monastic houses. The architecture of these new structures is called Romanesque because it came from Roman models. Its arches were rounded on top in the Roman fashion. William the Conqueror brought this style to England from Normandy.

Wealthy individuals often admitted that their donations were made to ensure their salvation: "This, however, I do first for the love of our Lord and God, second for the salvation of my father and mother, third for the safety of my sons," wrote one French donor. Regardless of the motives for their contributions, people felt that they could expect certain things of the clergy and the church. They demanded that the clergy be educated, unmarried, and well behaved. They also wanted the papacy, the office of the pope, reformed. Emperors since Charlemagne's time had claimed the right to reform the papacy whenever it became mixed up in their fights. The German emperor, acting in the spirit of religious renewal, appointed better-educated men as popes.

But the clergy wanted to elect their own pope, and for that purpose a monk named Hildebrand developed a system called the College of Cardinals. Based on the old custom of having priests elect their new bishop, the College of Cardinals—which still exists—gathered a group of high church officials called cardinals to vote for a new pope whenever a pope died. Hildebrand's plan removed the emperor from the process of choosing a pope. Ironically, when Hildebrand himself became Pope Gregory VII in 1073, the College of Cardinals did not elect him. He was so popular in Rome that the clergy and people alike proclaimed him pope.

"Bishop [Pope] Gregory, servant of the servants of God, to King Henry, greeting and apostolic [papal] benediction—that is, if he be obedient to the apostolic [papal] chair as beseems a Christian king."

—Letter from Pope Gregory VII to Henry IV, king and emperor of Germany, warning the king to respect the authority of the papacy, December 1075

Pope Gregory's contemporaries described him as a small man with a weak voice, but he had a strong vision of what the papacy should be. The pope, in Gregory's view, was the voice of Saint Peter (the founder of the first church in Rome) on Earth, and he had to answer to Saint Peter and to God for the sins of humans. It was the pope's duty to chastise any sinner—even an emperor. This belief brought Gregory into direct conflict with the emperor of the day, Emperor Henry IV of Germany.

In Gregory's eyes, Henry IV was a sinner because he continued to appoint bishops and abbots in Germany and to invest bishops with the symbols of their spiritual office: the bishop's staff and ring. Only the pope or his representative was supposed to conduct that sacred ceremony, called investiture. New rules of the church said that no one who was not a clergyman, not even the emperor, could perform investiture. By 1075, Gregory felt powerful enough to strike against Emperor Henry. He wrote several letters to Henry—calling him "beloved son"—praising the emperor for not selling church offices and for upholding the principle of an unmarried clergy, but attacking him for appointing abbots and investing bishops. The letters grew bitterer as Gregory emphasized his spiritual power over Henry.

Henry responded with a letter of his own, addressed to his bishops. In it he called Gregory "not pope but false monk." Gregory, said the emperor, had taken the papal throne

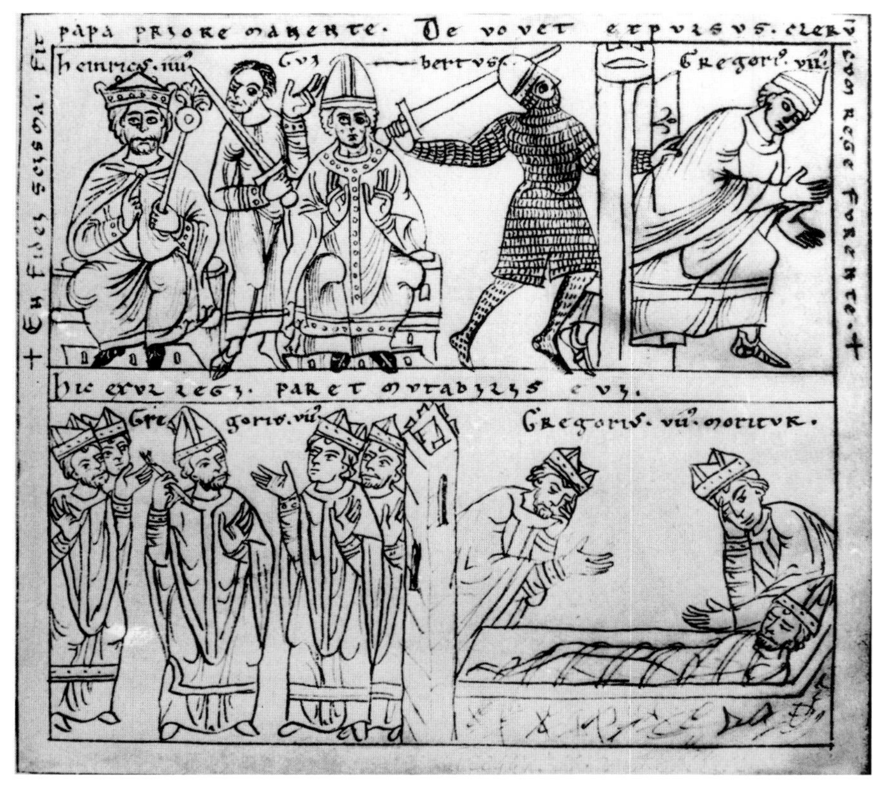

Pope Gregory VII excommunicates Henry IV (top left); Henry overpowers Gregory (top right) and brings in a new pope; Gregory again excommunicates Henry (bottom left); Gregory dies (bottom right). Their struggles were part of the great battle over who should have more power, the pope or the king.

"I, Henry, King by the grace of God, together with all our bishops, say unto you: Descend! Descend!"

—Letter from King Henry IV to Pope Gregory VII, asking the pope to abdicate the papal throne, January 1076

improperly; he was neither appointed by the king nor elected by the College of Cardinals. Henry argued that he too had a sacred trust from God—a monarch's duty to cleanse the church of a false pope.

Gregory sought allies among the German nobles and spoke of excommunicating Henry. Excommunication, a punishment that the church can use against its members, bans people from participating in the Christian religious community. In medieval times, it also dissolved feudal bonds of loyalty and forbade anyone from serving the excommunicated person. If the pope excommunicated Henry, the German nobles owed him no loyalty and could select anyone they wanted as their ruler.

Gregory excommunicated Henry in 1076. The nobles immediately met and declared that they would give Henry one year to make peace with the pope. If he did not, they would depose him. Unable to find loyal supporters among his nobility, the beleaguered emperor traveled to Canossa, in the Alps, where Gregory was staying. For three days, barefoot and clad in the rough wool garments of a repentant sinner, the emperor stood in the snow and cold outside the walls of the castle that housed the pope. Moved by Henry's tears and pleas and fearful of seeming too severe, Gregory finally relented. As pope, he could not refuse to absolve the sins of someone who was sincerely sorry, so he lifted the excommunication order.

Henry, however, had not given up the fight. He regained the loyalty of his nobles, and in 1084 he marched with his army into Rome and selected a new pope. Gregory died the following year, but Henry's triumph was not complete.

Papal reform had become too strong a movement for the emperor to control. Popes after Gregory continued to pressure Henry on the subject of investiture. A rebellion by German nobles deposed Henry in favor of his son, who ruled as Henry V. Finally, in 1122, the church persuaded Henry V to agree that only the clergy could invest bishops with the symbols of office and that the emperor could not appoint bishops and abbots. The bestowing of fiefs, though, remained the right of a king or an emperor.

GO EAST, PEOPLE

During the 12th century the papacy and monarchs brought more peace and stability to Europe, and the population grew. Trade flourished. Peasants and nobles alike sold their extra grain and spent their money. Some purchased practical items such as plowshares. Others bought luxury goods: silks, ribbons, and spices to add zest to bland food.

With the revival of trade and crafts, towns became an important part of the European landscape, as they had been in Roman times. They prospered throughout Europe, but nowhere more than in Italy. The Italian cities of Venice, Genoa, Pisa, Milan, and Florence became centers of trade and industry. Milan, which controlled overland trade with Germany, produced fine armor. Venice, Pisa, and Genoa were rivals in seagoing trade, both in the Mediterranean Sea and along the Atlantic coast to France, England, and the Netherlands.

Lords were so interested in attracting people to their towns that they offered to free peasants from serfdom if they would migrate to the towns. Other serfs took advantage of town laws that promised freedom to those who managed to live for a year and a day in town without their former masters claiming them. "Town air breathed free" is how they put it at the time. And as townspeople prospered, they also sought freedom from kings and bishops so they could govern themselves and make their own rules of trade and citizenship. Some rebellions against bishops were brutal. When the townspeople of one French city sought freedom, their bish-

In the 11th century, farmers grew more food than ever before in Europe. They had extra produce to sell, and trade increased. Markets, such as this one in which people barter for wine, corn, and eggs, bustled in the centers of many towns.

op hid in an empty wine cask in a basement, but they found him and killed him. As a final indignity, one man cut off the bishop's ring finger and stole his ring of office.

A new governing class arose in the towns in the 12th century. It consisted of the merchants who dealt in luxury items and large shipments of grain, wine, and dried fish. Unlike the nobility, whose wealth came from the land, the merchant class earned their wealth from trade—and they needed goods to trade. The growing demand for goods encouraged artisans to produce high-quality cloth, art, and other products. Peasants enjoyed the prosperity that came from bigger harvests, and sought better-quality shoes, plows, tools, and pottery. Skilled artisans flourished along with towns and markets.

"I, William, Count of the Flemings, not wishing to reject the petition of the citizens of St. Omer... grant them the laws and customs written below in perpetuity, and command that these laws remain inviolate."

—Charter granting self rule to the town of St. Omer, modern Belgium, 1127

In the late 12th century, due to the growth of Europe's population, people began moving into previously unsettled areas. When village populations outgrew their manors, lords urged serfs to clear forests and drain marshes, offering freedom to serfs who gave up their claim to land on the established manors and settled the new districts. During this period, Netherlanders began to settle the marshes bordering the North Sea, building dikes and windmills to drain these areas.

Around the same time, the German emperors conquered land in the Slavic east in an expansion called the Drive to the East. They encouraged people in the heavily populated Netherlands to migrate to territories along the Baltic Sea and in Hungary and Bohemia, the modern-day Czech Republic, bringing their technologies for draining marshes and plowing. Just as in the 19th-century United States the call to the adventurous was "Go west, young man," in the 11th and 12th centuries, agents of the German lords recruited serfs to go east. While William and his Norman lords were establishing their kingdom in England, the westernmost part of Europe, a different kind of migration took place on the eastern border, as peasant men, women, and children trudged into a new life in new lands.

In medieval Europe, more than 90 percent of the population worked on the land. Farmers rotated their crops in what is called a "three-field system": two fields were sown with crops in one year, while the third was left unplanted, to give the soil time to recover. The farmer in the center is broadcasting, or spreading, seeds from a basket.

CHAPTER 6

WORLDS IN COLLISION

THE *RECONQUISTA* AND THE CRUSADES

Europe's peasant population grew rapidly, both in the old territories and in newly settled lands. The noble population, though, grew even faster. Noble mothers, who ate more meat than peasant women (who ate mostly cereals), produced children who were more likely to survive the dangers of childhood diseases. The result was an ever-increasing number of ambitious, often aggressive young noblemen. They were a force to be reckoned with, as the sons of Tancred de Hauteville proved.

Tancred was a minor noble in Normandy. He had twelve sons, five by his first wife and seven by his second. He almost certainly had daughters as well, but we know nothing about them—their names and deeds were not recorded. The sons, though, made their mark in history. By law, only the eldest son could inherit Tancred's small ancestral estate. So the others set out to seek their fortunes elsewhere.

Three of the brothers—William Iron-Arm, Humphrey, and Drogo—became warriors, fighting sometimes as mercenaries (for pay) and sometimes as bandits (for themselves). Meanwhile, the new religious feeling sweeping across Europe had made pilgrimages to sacred sites popular with people of all classes, and the warrior brothers decided that they, too, should visit the holy city of Jerusalem in the late 11th century. On the way, they discovered that Sicily and southern Italy were fine places to practice their military skills. The Arabs and the Byzantine Greeks were fighting each other in these places, and both sides hired mercenaries.

Soon the remaining de Hauteville brothers had joined their kin, and the brothers began recruiting armies and carving out kingdoms of their own rather than fighting for local factions. Two of them, Robert Guiscard ("the Fox" or "the Sly") and Roger, conquered southern Italy and the island of Sicily. With the pope's approval, in 1072 they founded a Norman kingdom there that was similar to the state that William the Conqueror had just established in England, after his Norman Conquest. The de Hauteville family's ambitions didn't end there. One of their descendants, Robert's son Bohemund, soon impressed enemies and allies alike with his ruthlessness as a crusader and conqueror.

Like southern Italy, Spain also offered opportunities for younger sons of the European nobility. The Christians of Spain, joined by fighters from other parts of Europe, waged a long war against the Moors, as they called the Muslims who had ruled much of Spain since the early 8th century. In this fight, called the *Reconquista* (Reconquest), warriors from the Christian states tried to drive out the Moors and establish their own kingdoms in the reconquered territories. The *Reconquista* is the subject of the Spanish epic poem *El Cid.* The poem's hero is based on a real person, Rodrigo Díaz, who was born around 1043 in Castile, a kingdom in north-central Spain. Díaz was a nobleman—his nickname, *el Cid,* means "lord" in Arabic—and the poem portrays him as a popular champion of the Christian faith: "And forth to look upon him did the men and women throng. . . . As with

In this scene from the 1961 movie El Cid, *Charlton Heston as Rodrigo Diaz defends Spain against the Moors.*

one mouth, together they spake with one accord: 'God, what a noble vassal. . . .'" But in reality he was an opportunist who fought both Christians and Muslims, plundering churches and mosques alike.

CROSS OF THE SWORD

The turmoil of the *Reconquista* attracted adventurers, and in the long run it loosened the Muslim grip on Spain. By the early 12th century, the Muslims were beginning to lose control of the area that had been the westernmost province of the Arabs' empire and one of its chief centers of learning. As Muslim power slowly crumbled, the Christian kingdoms of Castile, Aragon, and Portugal began to expand.

The Arab world faced other troubles during this period. French and Norman nobles were creating new kingdoms and principalities, territories ruled by princes, in Sicily and Spain, eroding Arab rule. Meanwhile, the Seljuk Turks, a nomadic central Asian tribe who had converted to Islam, were making inroads on Arab territories in the East. The Turks conquered Baghdad, the heart of the medieval Arab world, and then moved west. Turning their attention from the Arabs to the Byzantine Greeks, they defeated the army of the Byzantine Empire and gained control of Byzantine territory in Anatolia (part of modern Turkey). They renamed this region Roum, an adaptation of "Rome."

The Turks' gradual conquests in the eastern Mediterranean brought Jerusalem and other parts of the Near East, modern Turkey, Syria, Lebanon, Jordan, Israel, Palestine, and Iraq, under Turkish control during the 11th century. This meant that Christians from western Europe making pilgrimages to the holy sites in Jerusalem were greeted at inns and shrines not by the tolerant Arabs but by the Turks, who were less hospitable toward Christians. As a result, pilgrimages became more difficult and dangerous. Byzantine Christians who lived in the eastern lands complained to the western pilgrims and clergy that the Turks persecuted them.

The Turkish conquest of Jerusalem and other parts of the remaining Byzantine Empire led to talk of cooperation

between the Byzantine emperor in the East and the pope in the West. Relations between the Byzantine and Roman churches were strained. Both considered themselves part of the same Christian faith. But they had clashed many times over the years over issues of religious practice, such as whether Christians should use two fingers or three to cross themselves, and over political issues, such as whether the pope in Rome was dominant over the patriarch, the head of the church in Constantinople. Finally, the two branches of the church had split. One became known as the Roman Catholic Church, the other as the Greek Orthodox. The Turkish threat, though, led the Byzantine emperor to call on the pope for help in defending Constantinople. The result was a clash of cultures called the Crusades.

By the 11th century, the Seljuk Turks, a tribe of nomads from central Asia, had begun invading Arab lands in the Near East and gained control of Byzantine territory in what is now Turkey. The armies engaged in fierce warfare, but the Byzantines lost many battles to the Turks.

An explosive combination of interests, ambitions, and religious feeling gave rise to the First Crusade in 1095. Pilgrims complained that the Turks were harassing them. Merchants of Italian towns said that the Turks interfered with their trade, and that the towns' economies were suffering as a result. After the Byzantine army suffered a defeat at Turkish hands, the Byzantine emperor, Alexius Comnenus, wrote to the pope in consternation, asking the pope to send mercenaries to his aid—perhaps some of those fierce and footloose Normans. Alexius hinted that in return for such help he would reunite the two churches.

In 1095, at a council of French clergy and nobility, Pope Urban II preached a sermon that was a stirring call to arms to liberate the Holy Land, current Israel and Palestine. He flattered the nobles, praising their fame as warriors, and called on them to avenge the Christians in the East. Muslim Turks had killed Christians, destroyed churches, and invaded the Byzantine Empire. But, Urban declared, the French noblemen could aid their fellow Christians and reclaim the Holy Sepulcher, the tomb in which Jesus had been buried, from the Turks.

The pope also mentioned overpopulation in France and pointed out that instead of fighting one another for land and fiefs, Frankish warriors could go to the Holy Land and carve out estates there. "This land which you inhabit," Urban told his listeners, "shut in on all sides by the seas and surrounded by the mountain peaks, is too narrow for your large population." He also promised that those who went on this holy crusade would be forgiven for all their sins and would be certain of going to heaven.

Urban's audience responded with enthusiastic cries of "God wills it!" But the pope realized that too much enthu-

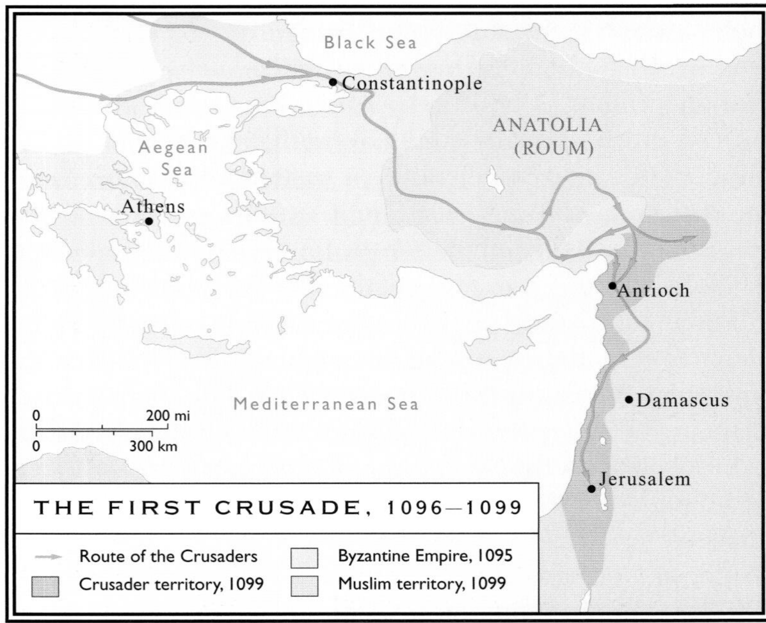

THE FIRST CRUSADE, 1096–1099

siasm would raise not an army but an unruly mob. He cautioned that "we neither command nor advise that the old or feeble, or those incapable of bearing arms, undertake this journey. Nor ought women to set out at all without their husbands, or brothers, or legal guardians. Let the rich aid the needy; and according to their wealth let them take with them experienced soldiers." Clergymen were not to go without the consent of their bishops.

Despite Urban's words of caution, his speech inspired a crowd of younger sons, peasants, poor knights, and members of the clergy. The pope knew that Emperor Alexius Comnenus had asked for a mercenary army of knights, but Urban could not raise an organized army out of this ragtag assembly. He wanted to send an army led by a king or high-ranking noble who could be counted on not just to win the Holy Land from the Turks but to place it under papal control. No king or major feudal lord, however, wanted to leave his own territory to pursue this far-fetched goal. Persuading the nobility to join up took some time. Finally, the adventurous and foolhardy Duke Robert of Normandy, son of William the Conqueror, agreed to go on the crusade. So did several other French and Norman nobles, including Bohemund, son of Robert Guiscard and grandson of Tancred de Hauteville.

In this late 14th-century illustration, Pope Urban II makes a stirring speech to French nobles. He called on them in 1095 to help save the Byzantine Empire from the encroaching Turks. This so-called holy war would become the First Crusade.

CRUSADE, TAKE ONE

The First Crusade was really two crusades: a main army of knights and nobles, and a popular crusade. The popular (meaning "of the people") crusade was a mob of peasants and clergy led by an impoverished knight, Walter the Penniless, and a preacher, Peter the Hermit. According to the New

About 25,000 men marched on foot from Europe to Asia Minor in the first popular crusade led by Peter the Hermit. The Turks killed almost all of them in a surprise attack near the ancient city of Nicaea in modern Turkey.

Testament, Christ would one day return to Earth and take his followers to join him in Heaven: "In my Father's house are many rooms; if it were not so, I would have told you. I am going there to prepare a place for you. And if I go and prepare a place for you, I will come back and take you to be with me that you also may be where I am." Walter and Peter's followers believed that the year 1100 would bring this Second Coming of Christ, and they wanted to be in Jerusalem when it happened.

An Arabic Cry to Arms against Crusaders

AL-AHIR, ACCOUNT OF THE FIRST CRUSADE, 12TH CENTURY

Ibn Al-Athir, a Persian intellectual, wrote a history of the Muslim world from its beginnings until his own day. Born in 1160, Al-Athir relied on earlier accounts of the events surrounding the First Crusade, which took place in the late 11th century. He did, however, have his own experiences fighting against the crusaders, especially with the Turkish ruler Saladin and in the Third Crusade of Richard III. He wrote his history in verse, expressing great sorrow at the brutality of battle, but calling Islamic soldiers to defend their territory.

We have mingled blood with flowing tears, and there is no room left in us for pity
To shed tears is a man's worst weapon when the swords stir up the embers of war.
Sons of Islam, behind you are battles in which heads rolled at your feet.
Dare you slumber in the blessed shade of safety, where life is as soft as an orchard flower?
How can the eye sleep between the lids at a time of disasters that would waken any sleeper?
While your Syrian brothers can only sleep on the backs of their chargers, or in vultures' bellies!
Must the foreigners feed on our ignominy, while you trail behind you the train of a pleasant life, like men whose world is at peace?
When blood has been spilt, when sweet girls must for shame hide their lovely faces in their hands!
When the white swords' points are red with blood, and the iron of the brown lances is stained with gore!
At the sound of sword hammering on lance young children's hair turns white.
This is war, and the infidel's sword is naked in his hand, ready to be sheathed again in men's necks and skulls.
This is war, and he who lies in the tomb at Medina [Muhammad] seems to raise his voice and cry: 'O sons of Hashim!
I see my people slow to raise the lance against the enemy: I see the faith resting on feeble pillars.
For fear of death the Muslims are evading the fire of battle, refusing to believe that death will surely strike them.'
Must the Arab champions then suffer with resignation, while the gallant Persians shut their eyes to their dishonor?
May Almighty God show mercy to his soul
And grant unto him forgiveness for his sins.

While the main army got organized, gathered supplies, and negotiated with Italian merchants for ships, the mob set off by foot across Europe. Some in this group argued that they didn't have to go to the Holy Land to fight those who were not Christians; they could do just as well by attacking Jews in Europe. The first pogroms—persecutions in which Jews were rounded up, robbed, killed, and burned—occurred in the German city of Cologne.

Most of the popular crusaders, however, continued through Hungary and the Balkan Peninsula. When they finally reached Constantinople, Emperor Alexius was so disgusted with them that he forced them to camp outside the city, where they committed petty thefts. Eventually, the emperor agreed to ferry them across the Bosporus, the waterway between Constantinople and Asia Minor. After the popular crusaders landed, the Turks attacked and killed most of them, although Peter the Hermit managed to escape to Constantinople.

In the meantime, the main army of crusaders gathered in Constantinople. Relations between Emperor Alexius and the westerners were not cordial. Anna Comnena, Alexius's daughter, left a fascinating account of how the Byzantines saw the crusaders. Anna claimed that the crusaders could not be trusted, writing, "There were among the Latins such men as Bohemund and his fellow counselors, who, eager to obtain the Roman Empire for themselves, had been looking with avarice [greed] upon it for a long time." Anna was right about Bohemund.

She described one time when her father invited Bohemund to a feast. Knowing that Bohemund would be suspicious, the emperor had his cooks bring raw meat to his guest and told Bohemund to have his own cooks prepare it if he preferred. In a generous gesture, Bohemund gave all the prepared banquet food to his followers. The next day he asked them how they were feeling to find out if the meal had been poisoned. They felt fine. Bohemund had been willing to risk their lives, not his own. Devious himself, he was suspicious of others. "Such a man was Bohemund," wrote Anna. "Never, indeed, have I seen a man so dishonest.

In everything, in his words as well as his deeds, he never chose the right path." And, as events would soon show, Bohemund was hungry for power.

After many squabbles, Emperor Alexius and the crusaders reached an agreement. He would supply provisions for their war against the Turks, and they would return to him the cities of Asia Minor that the Byzantine Empire had lost to the Turks. With Alexius's help, the crusaders moved into the Turkish-occupied territory. They revealed their true intentions as soon as they captured the first of the Turkish-held cities. Instead of turning it over to Alexius as they had agreed, they made him pay for it.

The crusaders' resolve was tested in 1098, when they besieged the city of Antioch in modern Turkey. They spent

The crusaders quelled the Turks in this pitched battle outside the walls of Antioch, Syria, in 1098. The Christian soldiers continued on to fight an even more grizzly battle to take Jerusalem. (The face on the shield, at left, is an embellishment of the artist.)

"When one comes to recount cases regarding the Franks, he cannot but glorify Allah (exalted is he!) and sanctify him, for he sees them as animals possessing the virtues of courage and fighting, but nothing else."

—Usamah Ibn-Munqidh, an Arab gentleman, from a personal history, 1175

the winter camping outside the well-fortified city. Emperor Alexius had cut off their supplies. As food grew short, their situation grew desperate. Finally, in the spring, an Italian fleet brought supplies, and the crusaders prepared to renew their attack.

One witness says that Bohemund suggested to his fellow crusaders: "if it seems good and honorable to you, let one of us put himself ahead of the rest, and if he can acquire or contrive the capture of the city by any plan or scheme... let us with one voice grant him the city as a gift." But the clever Bohemund had already made contact with a Christian inside the city walls who let him climb up at night and open the gates for the crusading army. The crusaders were victorious, but their victory was short-lived. The Turks soon regrouped and sent a large force against the crusaders occupying Antioch. Now the crusaders were trapped between a force of Turks who still held a castle in the city center and another force camped outside the city walls. Starving, they were reduced to eating rats. Bohemund saw one way out: an attack on the Turks outside the city. The crusaders won this battle—and Bohemund claimed the city for himself.

Bohemund's claim so enraged the other nobles that the crusade nearly fell apart. But the leaders settled their differences and continued to their goal, Jerusalem, which they captured in the summer of 1099. It was a terrible battle. One eyewitness said there was so much blood in the streets that it came up to the horses' knees.

What, the noble leaders of the crusade wondered, should they do with Jerusalem? The petty fighting and land-hunger that had marked their earlier conquests seemed inappropriate in the holy city itself. In the end, they named the only nobleman who had come on the crusade for genuine religious reasons as the first king of Jerusalem.

The First Crusade established the Latin Kingdom of Jerusalem as well as several other Near Eastern principalities, which were granted to nobles who had taken part in the great fight. One of those nobles, of course, was Bohemund, who finished the crusade as prince of Antioch, a title he passed on to his descendants. And although the crusaders' conquest of the Arab and Turkish population had been bloody, as Christians and Muslims lived together they became economically dependent on each other and shared many customs. Newcomers from Europe were often surprised by how well they got along.

Colonizing Jerusalem and the surrounding lands had an enormous impact on Europe. The crusaders returned home with a better knowledge of building stone castles and the machines that could besiege them, a taste for more highly spiced foods, and an appreciation for luxurious silk and cotton garments. They also brought home many relics, items considered sacred because they were said to date from the early days of Christianity. These gains influenced life in Europe, even while more crusades surged eastward in the centuries that followed. In spite of their victories in the Near East, Europeans were always a minority there, in danger of being overwhelmed by the Arabic-speaking armies that sought to regain control of the region. Western Europe would have to make repeated efforts to keep Jerusalem in Christian hands.

Among the valuable goods that crusaders brought back from the East were pieces of saints' bodies, or relics. These were thought to be holy and were encased in precious metals.

CHAPTER 7

LADIES, LOVERS, AND LIFESTYLES

THE FLOWERING OF MEDIEVAL CULTURE

Eleanor of Aquitaine was a teenager when she got married in 1137. It was no ordinary wedding—the groom was the king of France. In fact, Eleanor's life was extraordinary from beginning to end. She lived in a time of new ideas, rising wealth, and passionate outbursts of faith and emotion. During the 11th and 12th centuries, medieval culture changed in ways that touched the lives of everyone from nobles to peasants. Eleanor didn't just experience those changes; she helped to inspire some of them.

Romance and the arts surrounded Eleanor as she grew up in the duchy of Aquitaine in southwestern France. Her grandfather, Duke William, had been known throughout France for his love affairs and the poetry he wrote. When Eleanor was in her teens, her father died, and she became duchess of the large fiefdom of Aquitaine. But, before he died, her father had arranged for her to marry the king of France. The French kings were always looking for heiresses to marry in order to bring more land and wealth under royal

Children play a game called frog-in-the-middle in an illustration from a medieval manuscript. As Europeans became wealthier in the 11th and 12th centuries, nobles had more leisure time. Traveling acrobats and entertainers amused children of all classes.

> *"I have voluntarily sworn that I will never take a husband without the advice, consent, and wish of my lord, Philip, king of France, and that I will place under his guardianship my daughter."*
>
> —Contract made by Blanche of Champagne, a French noblewoman, with her lord, King Philip II of France, 1201

control, and marriage to the young duchess of Aquitaine was a rare opportunity. No one asked Eleanor what she thought about it, but she kept the agreement and married the young king, Louis VII.

The marriage was not a happy one. Eleanor came from a sophisticated, worldly court in warm southern France. She disliked the damp chill of Paris. More important, she had little in common with her husband. Louis had been raised to join the clergy and was more like a priest or a scholar than a knight. He wasn't even supposed to be king—he inherited the throne when his older brother died. "I thought to have married a king," Eleanor is reported to have said, "but I married a monk."

Real trouble between the royal couple began when Louis went on the Second Crusade to the Holy Land. By that time, Eleanor had given birth to two daughters but no son to inherit the throne, so she decided to accompany her husband on the crusade, hoping to conceive an heir along the way. Dressed as female warriors, she and several other noble French ladies set off in high spirits. Such bold behavior caused a scandal, but worse was to come. When the couple reached Antioch, they met Eleanor's uncle, Raymond, a handsome man and a great warrior. Eleanor left the crusade to stay with Raymond, and rumors spread that the two were lovers. Whatever the truth of that story, Eleanor had not produced a male heir by the time she and Louis returned to France. Louis asked the French bishops to annul, or cancel, their marriage. (The Catholic Church did not allow couples to divorce.) The marriage was

A lady is either hoisting her lover to her tower window or lowering him to the ground. With more time for leisure, the lords and ladies of the courts were able to indulge a romantic interest in the emotions of love.

dissolved, and Eleanor, now 30 years old, was no longer queen of France.

She was still the duchess of Aquitaine and a desirable marriage partner. Henry, the 18-year-old count of Anjou and duke of Normandy, had met Eleanor in Paris. Now he sought her hand. Despite the age difference, the match had advantages for each. By marrying Eleanor, Henry would become duke of Aquitaine. And by marrying Henry, Eleanor would become the wife of a man who was in line to become king of England. The two were wed in 1152, eight weeks after Eleanor's marriage to Louis ended.

The marriage was a painful blow to Louis. Henry was his greatest rival, the most powerful vassal in France—and the most rebellious. Together, Henry's fiefs were larger than the territory Louis controlled. As a further wound to Louis's dignity, Eleanor bore Henry four sons. A mighty feud arose between Henry and Louis.

Henry spent a lot of time traveling through his French fiefs and in England. Eleanor tended to their interests in Aquitaine. In Poitiers, the capital of Aquitaine, she headed one of Europe's most cosmopolitan courts, a center of art, learning, and style that gave birth to knightly literature and manners. Eleanor's court was part of a sweeping trend: Europeans were developing more refined tastes, and intellectual life was taking on new vitality.

LOVE CONQUERS ALL (UNLESS YOUR NAME IS ABELARD)

Contact with the Arab world brought some of the changes in taste. From the Arabs of Spain, Europeans learned to appreciate lyrical poetry, which was about the emotions, especially love. At the same time, warfare in Europe decreased because younger sons of nobles found more profit in fighting for territory outside Europe. Peace and refinement changed the medieval knight. Once a rough warrior, he now became a courtier, a term applied to young men who knew how to behave politely in a lord's court. The new standards of knightly behavior and military virtue came to be called chivalry, from the French word *chevalier,* meaning "mounted warrior." The code of chivalry called for a knight to be courageous, loyal, trustworthy, generous to a conquered foe, and eager to defend the Christian faith. Noblewomen became objects of respect and elaborate courtesy. Nowhere was this more evident than at the court of Eleanor of Aquitaine.

Eleanor herself was highly cultivated. She was familiar with the romantic traditions of her poet grandfather, the learning of Parisian philosophers, the ways of Norman and English nobility, and the exotic culture of the East. Poets and nobles flocked to her brilliant court. Their lives of leisure and interest in the refined life produced *courtoisie* (meaning "courtesy"), a new standard of politeness, including behavior in love. Men were taught how to speak to ladies and were punished in a "court of love" if they offended a woman.

New literary works celebrated the changing relations between noblemen and ladies—the passionate, worshipful attitude toward women that came to be called courtly love. Poets wrote lyrical poetry, such as this stanza, to celebrate the women they adored:

I sing of her, yet her beauty
is greater than I can tell,
with her fresh color, lovely eyes,
and white skin, untanned
and untainted by rouge.
She is so pure and noble
that no one can speak ill of her.

They also wrote longer tales called romances, about heroes and heroines whose love was tested by separations and adventures. Many of these romances centered on the legendary figure of King Arthur. In early stories, Arthur was described as a British king who fought off Saxon invaders. Later, Arthur's legend grew more elaborate. Stories of the adventures of his

In this illustration on a 15th-century shield, a knight has removed his helmet to present himself to his lady love. The words "You, or Death" are inscribed on the ornamental shield, which was made for use in parades, not combat. It may have been presented as a prize to the winning contestant in a tournament.

Romance in the Earl's Dining Hall

AN ENGLISH NOBLE, BLONDE OF OXFORD, 13TH CENTURY

In the 13th-century romance, Blonde of Oxford, *the hero, Jehan de Dammartin, is a squire to the earl of Oxford. As a squire, it was his duty to serve the earl's dinner guests, including Blonde, the earl's beautiful young daughter. The story takes place in England even though the author, who is unknown, wrote in French. But English nobles spoke French, and were very much a part of the French tradition of courtly love that encouraged writing of romances to explain the behavior expected between a man and a woman in love.*

Fair, and fairer still than I can say, was Blonde the Earl's daughter. She sat at dinner, and was served by Jehan, fair and free of body, who pained himself much to earn all men's grace by his courteous service. He waited not on his lady alone, but up and down throughout the hall; knight and lady, squire and page, groom and messenger, all he served according to their desire, and thus from all he earned good-will. He knew well to seize the moment for serving and honoring each guest, so that Blonde, the fair and shapely, found her needs none the worse supplied.

After the dinner they washed their hands, and went to play.... Jehan went with whom he would; and, on his return, oftentimes would he go to... countess's [chamber], wherein the ladies... kept him to teach them French. He, as a courteous youth... [He] knew all chamber-games—chess and tables and dice, wherewith he diverted the lady Blonde; often said he *check* and *mate* to her. Many other games he taught her; and taught her a better French than she had known before his coming; wherefore she held him full dear....

One day, as Blonde sat at table, it was for Jehan to carve before her.... By chance he cast his eyes on her; yet he had seen her daily these eighteen weeks past.... From this look such thoughts came into his head, that on his carving he thought no more. Blonde, who marked his thoughts astray, took upon her to rebuke him, and bade him think on his carving.... "Carve, Jehan, are you sleeping or dreaming here? I pray you, give me now to eat; of your courtesy, dream now no more." At this word Jehan... seized the knife as a man in a dream... but so distraught was he that he cut deep into two fingers.

Knights of the Round Table were added to it. The unlawful love of his queen, Guinevere, for Lancelot, one of his vassals, formed the subject of much medieval literature.

Courtly manners were displayed at tournaments, war games that were based on real combat. Knights on horseback charged each other on a field laid out for the fight. They tried to knock each other off their horses. When one was down, they resumed the combat on foot, fighting with swords until one surrendered. Nobles organized tournaments to practice their fighting skills. A tournament might celebrate the knighting of a son, the marriage of a daughter, the crowning of a king, or the heroic entrance of a prince into a city. In fact, any excuse was a good one for these mock battles.

While poets rhymed and knights charged each other on horseback, a revival of learning took place. Students flocked to hear teachers lecture in Latin, the scholarly language of all Europe. The most sought-after teacher was Peter Abelard, born into a knightly family in Brittany, a province in western

Two mounted knights joust with lances across a wooden barrier at a medieval tournament. Tournaments were mock battles that were staged for the entertainment of the nobility. From raised seats ladies cheered for their favorite knights, who tested their combat skills in elaborate war games.

France, in 1079. He could have inherited his father's lands, but instead he became fascinated by theological and philosophical arguments. Abelard settled in Paris, the center for such debates, and soon developed a reputation as a thinker, with students who paid to hear his lectures.

Later in life, Abelard wrote his autobiography and called it *The History of My Misfortunes*—for good reason. While teaching in Paris, he was hired by a high official at Paris's great cathedral, Notre Dame, to tutor Héloïse, the official's bright, beautiful young niece. But Abelard's description of their lessons told that "Under the pretext of study we spent our hours in the happiness of love, and learning held out to us the secret opportunities that our passion craved." She became pregnant, and the couple faced a dilemma.

Jean de Meung told the story of the tragic love between Héloïse and Abelard, pictured here, in his celebrated lyric poem about courtly love from the late 13th century, Le Roman de la rose *(The romance of the rose).*

If they married, Abelard could not pursue a career in the church, because the clergy had to remain unmarried. Not wanting to ruin his career, Héloïse refused to marry him. But when their son was born, they secretly married. Not knowing that they were wed, Hélöise's uncle was outraged when he learned about the baby. He arranged for thugs to assault Abelard, who survived a brutal attack but retired to a monastery. Héloïse also withdrew to monastic life. Their child, a boy named Astrolabe, may have been raised by Abelard's father.

In time, both Héloïse and Abelard became heads of religious communities. Abelard's autobiography circulated widely, and after reading his account of their old love, Hélöise wrote to him, "I beg you to restore your presence to me... by writing me some word of comfort.... When in the past you sought me out for sinful pleasures your letters came to me thick and fast." She sympathized with Abelard's misfortunes but reminded him that she too had suffered.

In addition to new manners, poetry, and scholarship, the 12th century produced a new architectural style that modern art historians call Gothic. It shaped many medieval cathedrals. Like much else in medieval culture, Gothic architecture has a connection to Eleanor of Aquitaine. Suger, the abbot who arranged the marriage between Eleanor and Louis VII and later oversaw their kingdom while they were on the Second Crusade, was a major supporter, or patron, of the new architecture.

Because flying buttresses helped support Gothic buildings, walls could be thinner and windows larger and more numerous. Immense round windows, such as this one in the cathedral of Chartres, France, were filled with colored panes of glass arranged in symmetrical patterns. Called rose windows, they filled the interior of the church with soft light.

Gothic architecture departed in important ways from the earlier Romanesque style. The walls of Romanesque churches were built of heavy masonry as was typical of Roman buildings, too. The thick walls limited the height of the churches, as well as the number and size of windows. Gothic architecture took a different approach. Rather than placing all the weight of a roof on the walls, the builders created an external skeleton of ribs or arches, called flying buttresses. These helped support the weight of the roofs. The walls, freed from having to bear all the weight, could have bigger windows and more of them. The change was revolutionary. Within 50 years, builders all over Europe had abandoned Romanesque architecture for Gothic. But as with any change, the transition was not entirely smooth. Some calamities occurred—faulty engineering could cause the whole roof of a church to collapse.

Building a cathedral was a complex undertaking that often took centuries. Some say, in fact, that cathedrals are never completed; new work is always added, or old work mended. A cathedral started with a bishop and his clergy, who financed the project. Some bishops invested the church's revenues in cathedrals. Pious patrons gave money for windows, bells, and maintenance. The bishop then hired an architect to design the building and do much more. As foreman of the project, the architect hired master

A furrier shows a sample of his wares to a customer in a detail from a stained-glass window in Chartres. Mullions, slender bars of iron, kept the colored panes in place. Skilled craftsmen etched scenes in the colored glass that told religious stories, traced dramatic events in history, and portrayed moments in their everyday lives.

masons, carpenters, stonecutters, sculptors, and carvers. Master craftsmen designed and supervised each stage of the project, down to casting the metal bells and making the stained-glass windows, but apprentices and less-skilled craftsmen did most of the work. Many unskilled laborers dug the foundations, carried the stones, set up the scaffolding, and performed other heavy work.

PLAY NICE AND SHARE YOUR TRENCHER

The 12th and 13th centuries must have been golden years for architects, masons, carpenters, and even laborers. Growing towns built walls around their edges, partly to protect themselves but also to show civic pride. Wealthy merchants and clergy built houses in the towns and nobles built castles in the countryside. A 12th-century castle was far more complex than the original motte-and-bailey structure.

The motte became a central stone tower called a keep, designed to be defended from attack. Walls as thick as 15 feet extended below ground, creating basement rooms that served as dungeons or prisons. The next level up had store-rooms for barrels of wine, flour, salted fish, and other provisions, perhaps also a guardroom and rooms for storing weapons. On the main level was the great hall, the center of castle life. Everyone took their meals in the hall, and many people slept on its floor after the tables had been put away for the night. The lord of the castle governed and entertained guests in the great hall, and he and his family lived in the upper stories.

Castles were defensive structures, but because they were so effective, few of them were attacked. The best way to assault a castle was to lay siege, surrounding the castle and cutting off its food supplies—and its water, too, if it did not have its own well. After the Crusades, machines for attacking castles became more common. One such machine was a battering ram, which could break down the gate. Ladders and movable wooden towers let attackers scramble over the castle walls. Another effective tactic against castles' fortifications was to sap, or dig under, the walls so that they would eventually collapse.

When castles were not under attack, which was most of the time, life in them was fairly comfortable. Wells provided drinking water. Water for washing came from a cistern, a tank on the roof that collected rain. Pipes carried water from the cistern through spigots into washbasins, called lavatories,

"I, Jörg Von Ehingen, knight, was sent in my youth as page to the Court of Innsbruck. . . . After a time I became carver and server of the dishes to [the queen of Austria]."

—Jörg Von Ehingen, who came from a distinguished family, describes his training as a youth in his autobiography written in the 15th century

Skilled masons build the towers of a castle stone by stone. Medieval stonemasons moved from town to town, often with their apprentices, finding work wherever a new building project was underway.

in the living quarters and the great hall. The castle's latrines might flow into chutes within the walls, or they might be outside the keep and drop directly to the ground or into the moat. One English king left a vivid record of his plumbing problems when he begged his engineers "for the love of God" to fix the latrines in a castle he visited frequently—the cold updrafts and their odor were unbearable.

Noble children who grew up in castles were not necessarily raised by their parents, who might be away at other castles, on crusade, or at the king's court. Nurses fed and entertained them. When children were seven or eight, their parents usually sent them to live with another noble family of high status, a custom called fostering. In their temporary new homes, young people learned court manners. Boys and girls learned to ride and to hunt, to wash their hands before coming to the table, to eat properly with their fingers (forks had not yet come into use), and to share their trencher (a piece of rough bread that served as a plate) with their dinner partner. They were not to "make a noise as you sup," wrote the author of *The Young Children's Book,* or to throw their bones to the dog. "Make neither the cat nor the dog your fellow at the table."

Girls and boys were treated much the same when young, but later they were trained for different roles. Young women spent most of their time in the castle's women's quarters, learning to sew and embroider, read romances and lyric poetry, play musical instruments and cards, and dance. Young men became squires, knights in training, and learned to fight, practicing with the sword and lance. Some young squires accompanied their lords to battles or on crusades. A squire became a knight in a special ceremony, usually when he reached the age of 21.

A young nobleman or noblewoman's future depended a lot on birth order. Younger children might be prepared for careers in church administration or monastic life, while older children, as heirs to their parents' property, generally married. Their parents or lords arranged their marriages, which were political or economic alliances between families. The two families often held intense negotiations about the marriage terms. The bride's family was expected to give the groom a dowry, or gift of property. Dowries could consist of land, jewels, gold and silver serving vessels, warhorses, armor, fine clothing—even armies.

A tall crest decorates the helmet of this Germanic knight. His shield, crest, and banner all have the same design, his coat of arms.(All nobles had a symbolic representation of their family and title on their armor.) His squire, a young man of the upper class whom the knight is training in the ways of arms and warfare, holds his horse.

Princess Philippa, who married the future King Edward III of England, brought to her marriage a dowry of boats and fighting men that the groom's mother used to invade England in his name. In exchange for the dowry, a husband's family promised a dower, a benefit for a wife if her husband died. It consisted of a third of his lands and estates. A wife could use the dower land for as long as she lived, and after her death it would go to their children.

Both marriages of Eleanor of Aquitaine, the godmother of courtly love, were arranged after much negotiation about dowries, dowers, and other terms. Her first marriage, to Louis VII of France, had been unsatisfactory to both partners. Her second, to Henry II of England, was at times stormy. Like many royal families, the family of Eleanor and Henry was torn by rival ambitions. At one point, Eleanor and one of her sons rebelled against Henry, with the support of France. As a result, Henry had Eleanor confined for more than a decade to a castle in England. After Henry's death, though, Eleanor again involved herself in politics and in the careers of two of her sons who became kings of England. She was still active at the age of about 80, when she led the defense of one of her castles against a siege by her own grandson. As her grandfather Duke William once wrote,

> I pray. . . that at my death
> all my friends will honor me,
> for I've known joy and gaiety
> in my domains and far away.

Eleanor truly experienced medieval life in all such fullness.

CHAPTER 8

RULERS AND REBELS

ROYAL AUTHORITY AND AMBITION IN ENGLAND, FRANCE, AND GERMANY

Henry II of England, the second husband of Eleanor of Aquitaine, was an energetic man. He exhausted his courtiers with administrative duties, hunts, combat in tournaments and battles, and the ruthless pursuit of his enemies. During church services, he fidgeted if he didn't have writing materials to jot down thoughts, plans, and orders. A muscular, freckled redhead, Henry had a fiery temper to match his ruddy appearance. His temper led to one of the most notorious acts of his reign—the murder of an archbishop—but his formidable energy helped him protect his possessions on the European mainland. Henry's efforts to hold and govern his kingdom were mirrored elsewhere in Europe during the 12th and 13th centuries, when monarchs gained power but also faced many challenges.

It all started with Henry II's grandfather, who was also named Henry and who was one William the Conqueror's

The king, queen, and courtiers—on raised platforms at back—have gathered to watch a tournament, or tourney. These pretend battles could turn deadly. During one fight in Cologne, Germany, more than 60 knights were killed.

> *"Matilda was brought up from early childhood in a convent of nuns and grew up there to womanhood, and... had been seen walking abroad wearing the veil like the nuns.... Long after she had discarded the veil, the king fell in love with her."*
>
> —Eadmer, a monk living in Canterbury, on the childhood of Henry I's wife, Matilda, in his *History of Recent Events in England*, late 11th and early 12th century

three sons. When the Conqueror died, his oldest son got Normandy, and his second son got England. Henry, the third, just got cash. When the new king of England died from an arrow wound during a hunt, rumors said that Prince Henry, his younger brother, was responsible. However it happened, the prince became Henry I of England. Then his other brother died, so he also became duke of Normandy. As a French duke, he owed allegiance to the Capetian kings of France, who tried to rule the country from Paris. The French kings, though, had a hard time winning recognition and obedience from their powerful, wayward counts and dukes—of whom Henry I was the most troublesome.

As Henry approached death after 35 years on the throne, his one heir was his daughter, Matilda. Hoping to secure for her control of his French territories, Henry married Matilda to a powerful French count, his worst enemy, Geoffrey Plantagenet of Anjou. Henry forced his English and Norman vassals to accept Matilda as queen, and before he died he had the satisfaction of knowing that she had a son named Henry.

After Henry's death, his vassals rebelled, unwilling to be ruled by a woman. After years of fighting, they finally agreed that her son—who had just married Eleanor of Aquitaine—would become King Henry II. His reign began the Plantagenet dynasty. Henry Plantagenet was king of England, but he also controlled, as vassal to the French king, half of France. Historians call this large territory the Angevin Empire after the county of Anjou in France owned by his father.

ORDER IN THE COURTS!

Since the time of William the Conqueror, the Norman kings of England had regarded the island realm as a convenient source of income—but not a fit place for a French-speaking Norman to live. Henry II was no different. Wanting to be free to defend his fiefs in France, he reorganized England so that its administration and judicial systems would run smoothly in his absence. As a result, England became one of

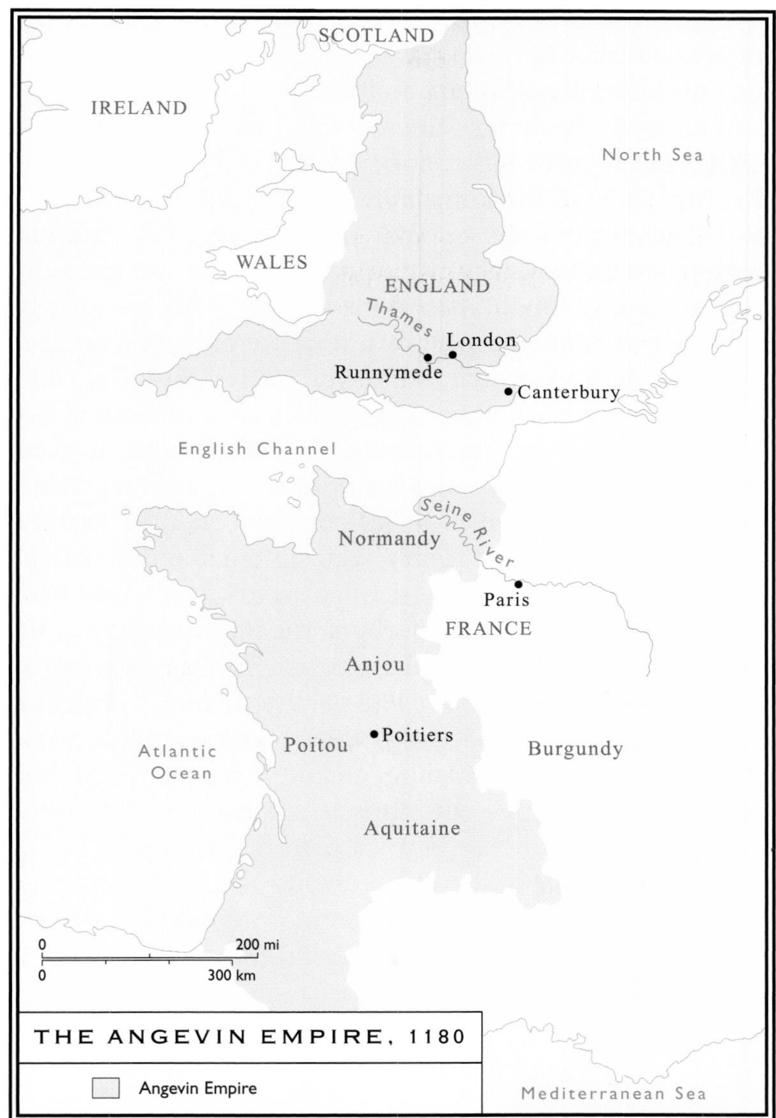

THE ANGEVIN EMPIRE, 1180

Europe's best-run kingdoms. Institutions that developed there later influenced the government of the United States.

One such institution was a system of circuit justices, officials who traveled through the kingdom to enforce royal laws. Henry encouraged people to seek solutions to land disputes by applying to these royal officials for judgment—and paying a fee to the crown for the decision. When a dispute arose over who owned a piece of land, the king's judges summoned the oldest, wisest, and best-informed men of the area to serve on an inquest, or inquiry, jury. The jury advised the judges about who had the better claim to the land. On the basis of their verdict, the judges settled the dispute, with the king's authority to back up their decision. The effective and popular system is an ancestor of the modern grand jury. The petty jury (from the French word *petit,* meaning "small") developed in the 13th century. Its task was to decide the guilt or innocence of people accused of crimes. Henry's overhaul of the judicial system was a success. It gave the kingdom a peaceful means of settling disputes, and it brought him revenue from the fees people paid.

It also led the king into an unexpected conflict with a bloody outcome.Thomas à Becket, the son of a London merchant, had served Henry well as chief officer of the Exchequer, the kingdom's treasury. Henry made this loyal follower archbishop of Canterbury, the highest office in the English church. But Becket seems to have had a strengthening of religious feeling when he was made archbishop, and afterward he sided with the church against his old friend and royal patron.

The dispute between king and church stemmed from the fact that the church had its own courts to settle cases concerning canon, or church, law. Henry insisted that clergy accused of felonies such as theft or homicide be tried in the royal courts, but Becket wanted them tried in the church courts by their bishops. The

The Exchequer, or treasury, was named for the checkered tablecloth that officials used as a sort of calculator to add up the fines they had collected for the king. A subject who didn't pay the fine was put in prison.

difference was significant—especially to the accused. A cleric convicted in a royal court of a felony would be hanged, but if convicted in a bishop's courts he need only say prayers or make a pilgrimage to atone for his wrongdoing.

To end the conflict, Henry exiled Becket to France, but the move was so unpopular with both the pope and the people that Henry had to bring him back, and the old fight resumed. Henry became so frustrated that he is said to have remarked to four of his knights, "Will no one rid me of this troublesome priest?" The courtiers, all too willing to fulfill their king's wish, went to Canterbury on a December evening and, in the middle of the cathedral, brutally killed the archbishop with a sword blow to the skull as he was praying. The slain Becket immediately became a martyr. Henry, forced to confess that his short-tempered remark had led to the death of his archbishop, atoned for his role in the murder by voluntarily submitting to a beating by monks.

A relief sculpture carved in alabaster shows Henry's men, with swords raised, on the verge of killing Thomas à Becket, the archbishop of Canterbury, who is at prayer in the cathedral. Henry was beaten after he confessed to wanting his archbishop killed.

Aside from his quarrel with Becket, most of Henry's energy went to safeguarding his French territories from his perpetual foes, the kings of France. Louis VII of France was Henry's enemy even before Henry married Eleanor, Louis's ex-wife. After Louis died, his son, Philip II Augustus, carried on the tradition of warring and plotting against the Plantagenets, rulers of England and the Angevin territories in France.

Upon Henry II's death, England and the Angevin territories went to Richard, Henry's third son with Eleanor, the older brothers having died. Richard was the queen's favorite son. He was a poet like Eleanor's grandfather and a chivalric figure who absorbed all the romantic ideals of his mother's court. He was also a fighter and a passionate leader of the Third Crusade to the Holy Land, where the Turks had unified under a charismatic leader named Saladin, who had captured Jerusalem. To combat this foe, the pope persuaded Richard's archenemy, Philip II Augustus of France, to join the crusade, along with a third monarch, Frederick I Barbarossa, emperor of Germany.

Thugs in the Cathedral

WILLIAM FITZSTEPHEN, LIFE OF THOMAS À BECKET, 1173–1175

William fitzStephen was a member of the English clergy and a close associate of Archbishop Thomas à Becket. In his biography of Becket, written between 1173 and 1175, he describes the archbishop's murder in Canterbury Cathedral as an eyewitness.

At the sight of these armed men, I say, the monks wished to close and bolt the door of the church. But the good archbishop, putting his whole trust in the Lord and refusing to be carried away by sudden panic at the onrush of the powers of evil, turned back and came down the steps, forbidding the monks to close the door, saying, "Far be it from us to turn the church of God into a fortress."... By this time those executioners came running in furious haste through the church door, finding it unexpectedly open.... On catching sight of the archbishop, these cut-throats at first drew back as though confused and bewildered, and abashed by his countenance. Then someone shouted, "Where is the traitor?" To this the archbishop made no reply. Then someone else said, "Where is the archbishop?" to whom he made answer, "Here am I, no traitor, but a priest of God....

A certain one struck him with the flat of his sword between the shoulders, saying, "Fly, you are a dead man." But the archbishop stood unmoved, and offering his neck [for a blow] commended himself to God.... With them also was Master Edward Grim, and he, putting up his arm [to ward off the blow] received the first stroke of the sword aimed at the archbishop's head. By this same stroke the archbishop was wounded in the head as he bent forward, and Grim in the arm.... Wiping off with his arm the blood that streamed from his head, the archbishop gave thanks to God, saying, "Into Thy hands, O Lord, I commend my spirit." As he knelt down, clasping and stretching out his hands to God, a second stroke was dealt him on the head, at which he fell flat on his face hard by an altar. He took care, however, and was granted grace, to fall in honorable fashion, covered down to the ankles with his pallium, [woolen band worn as symbol of church authority] as though in the act of prayer and adoration.

Frederick never reached the Holy Land—he drowned on the way while taking a swim. Philip hated fighting and disliked cooperating with Richard, so he decided to return to France. There, taking advantage of Richard's absence, he attacked Richard's fiefs. Richard, meanwhile, fought boldly in the Holy Land, earning the nickname Richard the Lion-Hearted. He captured a port city and reached an agreement with Saladin that Christians could visit Jerusalem on pilgrimage. Richard then returned to Europe to fight Philip, but died in his French territories from an infected arrow wound.

Philip II Augustus was a shrewd and successful monarch. His most significant exploit was against King John of England, brother of and successor to Richard the Lion-Hearted. John, the youngest son, had been groomed for a more comfortable life than defending his territories against a calculating enemy. He made a fatal blunder in marrying a young woman who was already engaged to one of King Philip's vassals. Claiming a feudal lord's right to protect his vassals' interests, Philip used John's marriage as an excuse to invade Normandy, Anjou, and Poitou (the northern part of the Angevin Empire). He met with little resistance and easily took over the valuable fiefs. By losing the territory, King John won the scornful nickname Lackland.

Philip wasn't King John's only opponent. Like his father, John ran into trouble with the archbishop of

Frederick I Barbarossa got his name from his red beard: "rossa" means "red" and "barbar" means "beard." His sons stand on either side of him, giving him advice. Frederick expanded German control into Italy. He drowned on the Third Crusade.

> *"On August 20 [1212], a certain German boy called Nicholas who had taken the crusader vow [hurried] to set out across the sea. He was accompanied by a great and countless multitude of German boys."*
>
> —Anonymous writer, description of the Children's Crusade, *Annals of Pacenza*, early 13th century

Canterbury—although a different archbishop, of course. The pope forced John to give the position of archbishop to the pope's candidate, Stephen Langton. Then, trying to win back his Norman territories from Philip, John lost a series of battles and desperately needed money for new military action. He forced the English nobility and townspeople to pay more taxes than ever before, and he insisted on turning a profit on every one of his feudal rights. For example, men had to pay John a fee to marry noble widows—unless the widows paid an even higher fee to escape being married. For a price, he also let guardians of noble orphans keep the orphans' property after they reached 21, the legal age of maturity, when they should have inherited their estates.

TALK AMONG YOURSELVES

Archbishop Stephen Langton led a revolt against these injustices. Nobles, townsmen, and knights banded together to defeat John at the battle of Runnymede, a meadow near the royal castle of Windsor, in 1215. They drew up a series of demands that King John reluctantly signed. The document is called the Magna Carta, Latin for "great charter." Most of it outlined John's abuses of his power over the nobility and of his feudal rights as king. The charter corrected abuses involving the remarriage of widows and the property of orphans. It also said that although the king could levy taxes that were customary, new taxes required the kingdom's consent.

The Magna Carta ensured that earlier judicial reforms would remain permanent. The townspeople, lesser nobles, knights, and free peasants strongly appreciated access to royal justice. By including in the Magna Carta a clause stating that "all free men shall be tried by a jury of their peers," the rebellious nobles and townspeople made certain that the jury system would continue.

Historians of law and government see the Magna Carta as the beginning of England's constitutional monarchy, a system of government in which the monarch is the head of state but with powers limited by the law. The Magna Carta stated that the king could not be above the laws of the land, but must abide by them. The Magna Carta's provisions evolved over time. The "jury of their peers" clause, for example, applied only to "free men" in the 13th century. It excluded women and unfree serfs. In the 20th century, however, the definition of citizenship expanded to include all adults. Getting King John to sign the Magna Carta was only half the battle. Getting him to keep his word would be more difficult. No one trusted him. But John I died the next year, from consuming too many peaches with cider. The throne went to his only son, Henry III, a child of nine. Because Henry was too young to rule, a group of nobles,

At the coronation of John I, one archbishop pours holy oil on him, while another places the crown on his head. Kings claimed that this ceremony gave them sacred powers that allowed them to overrule the church. The church disagreed.

> *"No free man shall be taken or imprisoned or dispossessed, or outlawed, or banished, or in any way destroyed, nor will we go upon him, nor send upon him, except by the legal judgment of his peers or by the law of the land."*
>
> —Magna Carta, England, 1215

churchmen, townsmen, and knights formed a council to rule according to the Magna Carta.

When Henry III came of age, he rebelled against the nobles and pursued his own policies. Throughout most of his long reign in the 13th century, he fought with his nobles, but particularly with Simon de Montfort. Simon had been a friend of Henry's and married his sister, but he organized resistance against his monarch. Simon and the other nobles gained power by asking the counties and towns to send representatives to meet and discuss questions of government. The meetings of these representatives and the nobles came to be called a parliament, from the French word *parler*, meaning "to talk." When the representatives gathered, they met separately from the nobles and powerful bishops and abbots. Eventually, these two groups became known as the House of Communes (or communities, today called Commons) and the House of Lords.

These meetings proved so useful for communicating and spreading information that when Edward I came to the throne after Henry III's death, he continued the practice. At first, Parliament did little actual decision-making. English monarchs called two elected representatives from each county and town to meet on special occasions. The king customarily called a meeting of Parliament when he planned to impose a new tax. Once the House of Commons approved the tax, the representatives could tell the people in their districts why it was necessary, and the people would be more likely to cooperate with the continued tax collectors. Parliament had become a convenience for the kings. In the 14th century, war with France forced the kings to call more frequently on the people for taxes. As the king's need for money increased, Parliament gained greater control over taxation and more say in how tax money was spent. It refused to grant more taxes, for instance, unless the king did a better job of prosecuting criminals and keeping peace in the countryside.

The Magna Carta and its enforcement changed the nature of government in England by forming representative institutions. Across the English Channel in France the kings saw the advantage of announcing their policies to representative bodies. These institutions developed at the local rather than the national level, because the traditional division of France into semi-independent provinces and fiefdoms remained strong. King Philip II Augustus also established a bureaucracy made up of professional lawyers to administer justice, collect taxes, and carry out his policies.

Meanwhile, the rulers of the German Empire pursued their own grand political ambitions. Although the empire had declined since the days of Charlemagne's heirs, Frederick I Barbarossa had come to the throne with dreams of making it great and influential once again. To do so, he needed more power. Looking back at the failures of earlier German emperors, he realized that in order to consolidate his power in Germany he would have to engage in long battles with other nobles, some of them his relatives. So he looked beyond Germany instead. Frederick acquired the duchy of Burgundy through marriage—then he turned his attention south, to Italy.

The towns of northern Italy had become very prosperous by the 12th century, but they were

English barons forced King John to sign the Magna Carta. His seal is attached to the original document. This was a crucial moment in English history because it was the first time a king agreed to come under the control of the law.

Banking began in Italy with money-lenders who did business on benches, or banks. They grew rich charging interest for their services. The man with the sack is borrowing money from lenders who are busy discussing, reading, and writing down the terms of the transaction.

rebellious and independent. It wouldn't be easy to conquer them or win them to his side. Still, Frederick went on the attack and his Italian campaign succeeded—only the city of Milan stubbornly resisted his siege. After three years Frederick captured the city, and threatened to destroy it entirely and salt the earth so that nothing would grow there. Frederick decided not to carry out his dire threat; instead, he spared Milan. He soon regretted that act of mercy, because Milan rallied a coalition of other cities and defeated Frederick's forces.

Frederick drowned on his way to the Third Crusade with Richard the Lion-Hearted. However, the Italian strategy did not die with him. It became part of the family policy. Frederick's son married the heiress of the kingdoms of Naples and Sicily in the hope of uniting Germany and southern Italy. Frederick Barbarossa died at the age of 32, but his son, Frederick, became one of the most remarkable figures in medieval history.

"[Frederick's] eyes are sharp and piercing, his nose well formed, his beard reddish, his lips delicate and not distended by too long a mouth. His whole face is bright and cheerful."

—Otto, bishop of Friesing, history of the reign of Frederick Barbarossa, 12th century

CHAPTER 9

EMPIRE ON EARTH, KINGDOM OF HEAVEN

POLITICS, POPES, AND RELIGIOUS CONFLICTS

Three key figures shaped the destiny of Frederick II of Germany. Two of them were his grandfathers. On his mother's side, Frederick was the grandson of the Norman king of Sicily. On his father's side, he was the grandson of Frederick I Barbarossa, the German emperor. Although both grandfathers died before Frederick was born in the late 12th century, they left him an impressive inheritance, passed down through his parents: the rule of Sicily and Germany and the imperial title.

The third influence on Frederick's life was very much alive. He was Pope Innocent III, who became Frederick's guardian when the boy was three, after the death of his father. Innocent was one of the most able, learned, and active of the medieval popes. He had pursued theology (the study of religion) at the University of Paris and church law at the University of Bologna, and he used his legal training in the church's political fights with the European monarchs. Innocent became pope in 1198 at age 37—young for the church's highest office—and accomplished much during his 18-year papacy.

Although the pope in Rome was his guardian, Frederick grew up in Sicily, his mother's homeland. The island's culture was a blend of Arabic, Byzantine Greek, and Latin traditions, and Frederick absorbed the learning of each group. He not only possessed a fine intelligence but—unlike most people during the Middle Ages—he was comfortable with people from all three cultures. Frederick was also curious about the natural world and interested in science. He traveled with a collection of animals that included ostriches, parrots, monkeys, leopards, panthers, lions, camels, a giraffe, and an elephant. He wrote a book, *On the Art of Hunting with Birds,* that talks about the study of birds, with information on hawks and other hunting birds drawn from his own observations. Frederick also conducted scientific experiments. One experiment tested how vultures find dead animals to eat. He placed hoods over their eyes, and when they could not detect meat near them, he concluded that they hunted by sight rather than smell.

Frederick's habit of independent thought carried over into politics. Pope Innocent III wanted Frederick to concentrate on ruling Germany, across the Alps from Italy and distant from papal affairs, rather than strengthening his power in southern Italy, where he might pose a threat to Rome. But by age 18 Frederick was already defying Innocent's successor, claiming the wealthy states of southern Italy as well as Milan and other cities near Rome. Fearful that Frederick would take over Rome, the pope reminded the young emperor that he had sworn to lead a crusade to Jerusalem.

Under pressure from Pope Gregory IX, Frederick finally embarked on a crusade—only to return to port complaining that his army was too sick to fight. Suspecting a lie, the pope excommunicated Frederick. The emperor, however, accomplished the goal of the crusade with diplomacy rather

King of Sicily and emperor of Germany Frederick II's book on falconry is still used by people who are training falcons to hunt game. Only nobles had the time and the money to keep falcons, which were expensive birds that required a lot of care.

than warfare, reaching a settlement with the Muslims who occupied Jerusalem. In return for granting Christians free access to Jerusalem, the Muslims could worship undisturbed by crusaders in their own mosques. Frederick, who understood Arabic, didn't hesitate to make a deal with the Arabs, but his success did not please the pope. Christians were not supposed to enter into treaties with Muslims, and the pope did not forgive Frederick. Undeterred, Frederick built an efficient, prosperous state in Sicily, where Christians, Jews, and Muslims lived together harmoniously, and left the German princes and cities to go their own ways.

SINK OR SWIM

When Frederick died in 1250, Germany was disunited, a patchwork of free towns, bishoprics (territories governed by bishops), and large duchies—a state of affairs that continued into the 19th century. But Frederick had made Sicily into a desirable possession, and the pope, not wanting a German to control it after Frederick's sons died without heirs, decided it should go to France. Neither the pope nor the French, however, considered two important factors. First, the Sicilians didn't want a French ruler. Second, King Peter of Aragon, a powerful kingdom in Spain, wanted the island for himself.

With the French unable to govern Sicily, Peter sent his fleet to take over. His fleet arrived just as a planned revolt against the French broke out on the island. On Easter Monday of 1282, as the church bells rang for the evening service known as vespers, Sicilian rebels massacred the French ruler's supporters. Some historians think that the Sicilian rebellion marked the birth of the Mafia. Peter of Aragon stepped into the civil strife and claimed Sicily for himself in defiance of the Pope.

The popes of the 13th century were concerned with more than international politics. In 1215—the same eventful year that saw Frederick II become king of Germany and King John of England sign the Magna Carta—Pope Innocent III called leading church figures to the Lateran Palace, the pope's residence in Rome, to reform church practices. Today only judges and juries determine whether an accused person is guilty or innocent, but in medieval Europe the clergy were a part of that process.

Until the Lateran Council, as Innocent's meeting came to be called, ordeals determined guilt or innocence. For example, in an ordeal by water, the person on trial was thrown into a body of water. Before the trial began, a priest blessed the water and asked God to allow the innocent to go unscathed. An innocent person would sink in the water—and was fished out and spared. The guilty would float, having been rejected by the blessed water, and were fished out to meet their punishment. The Lateran Council forbade priests from blessing the water so that the ordeal became meaningless. The council made many changes to such matters, as well as the Mass, marriage, and monastic orders.

One of the biggest problems the Lateran Council faced was heresy, the belief in ideas that the church declared to be false. The heretics who most disturbed the church were a group called the Cathari, which means pure. They are also known as Albigensians, from the town of Albi in southern France, where their movement was centered.

The Albigensians offered an answer to one of the most difficult questions in the Jewish and Christian faiths: If God is good, why does he permit evil? The Albigensian answer was older than Christianity. It said that there are two gods, one good and one evil, who struggle to possess souls. The

In the 1230s the church set up tribunals, or courts, in which churchmen judged people suspected of heresy. These tribunals were collectively known as the Inquisition. This etching from the 16th century shows a very public hearing. Usually trials were held in secret, and suspects often confessed to heresy under torture.

"[Inquisitor]: I know your tricks. What the members of your sect believe you hold to be that which a Christian should believe. But we waste time in this fencing. Say simply, Do you believe in One God..., the Son, and the Holy Ghost?"

—Bernard Gui, inquisitor at Toulouse, France, 1307–1323

god of good will ultimately win, and those who follow him will be saved, while those who follow the god of evil will be damned. To live a good life, the Albigensians said a person should give up worldly living, meat, and sex in order to lead a more spiritual life. A few Albigensians—called *perfecti* or perfect ones—managed to follow this strict rule. When Albigensians were dying, they asked for one of the *perfecti* to stand at their bedside to speed salvation.

The Albigensians' alternative to church doctrine appealed to many people, and by the beginning of the 13th century their movement had grown large enough to alarm the pope. According to a churchman named Raynaldus, "They so far annulled the sacraments of the Church... to teach that the water of holy Baptism was just the same as river water, and that the Host of the most holy body of Christ did not differ from common bread." A ruling by a church council was not enough to combat such heresies—the pope wanted the heretics to see the error of their beliefs. New religious orders, or brotherhoods of priests and monks, sprang up to give spiritual and intellectual guidance to the heretics. The pope gave these new orders his blessings.

FRIAR, FRIAR

One such order was founded by a Spanish priest named Dominic, who received an excellent education in the mixed Jewish, Arab, and Christian environment of his homeland before traveling to Rome. At the height of the Albigensian crisis, Pope Innocent III asked Dominic to preach against the heretics in southern France. Despite Dominic's reputation as a preacher and a priest who led a devout life, he won few converts at first, so he organized volunteers into an order to preach to heretics and unbelievers. The religious group he founded was called the Order of the Friar Preachers, or Dominicans, as they are called today.

Unlike earlier orders, the Dominicans did not retreat to monasteries. They lived among the poor, preaching to curious city people, arguing with heretics, and teaching at the universities, which were new institutions in the Middle Ages. Rather than living on the proceeds of manors, as monastic orders did, the Dominicans solicited donations from pious laypeople to support their preaching. With their learning and their example of living in poverty like Jesus' apostles, the Dominicans succeeded in converting some Albigensians.

Dominic may have succeeded with the Albigensians because his austerity matched, or even surpassed, theirs. His diet consisted of meager bits of dried fish, a little bread, and soup. The women who prepared his meals testified that he never ate more than two eggs and always watered down his wine. His wardrobe wasn't any more forgiving; he wore a

Pope Innocent II, flanked by two cardinals in flat red hats, has given an audience to Francis of Assisi (kneeling at right) and his monks. The Franciscans are dressed in simple brown robes held together with ropes, and their hair has been shaved in a style called a tonsure.

rough, hair shirt and an iron chain around his waist, and he only wore shoes in town. And for a bed, he chose the floor, preferably in the chapel. Explaining his humble existence to a pompous bishop, Dominic said, "heretics are more easily won over by examples of humility and virtue than by external display or a hail of words."

While Dominic organized an order of preachers against heresy, the son of a prosperous cloth merchant in central Italy won hearts and captured imaginations with a different sort of devotion. As a young man, Francis of Assisi, a town in central Italy, led a carefree, comfortable life. He was interested in courtly manners and revelry, not business or religion. One night in his early twenties, he had given a banquet for some friends. The revelers moved into the street—singing and waving torches and flowers. Francis, however, separated from them and was later found in a religious trance. This was the first in a series of events that led to a religious conversion.

He exchanged clothing with a beggar and began giving away the family money. To stop Francis's erratic behavior, his father disinherited him. The cloth merchant may have saved the family fortune, but he could not change Francis, who moved to the edge of Assisi to live with the poor. Francis had once heard a sermon in which priests were urged to "Cure the sick, raise the dead, cleanse the lepers, drive out devils. Carry neither gold not silver nor money in your belts or bag, nor two coats, nor sandals, nor staff, for the workman is worthy of his hire." He took those words as his guide and began preaching, even though he was a layman, not a priest.

When Francis had about a dozen followers, he sent them to Rome to request the pope's blessing on his preaching. Innocent granted the request—he must have seen the pious young Francis as the church's answer to the Albigensians' *perfecti*. Like the Dominicans, the order Francis established was a mendicant, or begging, order. In 1223 Francis wrote what became the official rule of the Franciscans. He advised that "The brothers shall appropriate nothing to themselves, neither a house, nor a place... they shall confidently go seeking for alms. Nor need they be ashamed, for the Lord made Himself poor for us in this world." This poverty, he told the brothers, "has made you poor in possessions, [but] has exalted you in virtues."

Francis's followers strove to imitate the life of Christ. Their very name, Friars Minor, meaning "little brothers," showed the cheerful humility that was their ideal. Francis became associated with animals—he is said to have preached even to them. His order drew a vast following, including many women, but although men could beg, the

text continues on page 134

Saint Francis preached a gentle message of love and caring for the poor. It was said that he cared so much for all beings that he even preached to the birds, as he is doing in this painting by Giotto di Bondone. Giotto was a noted 14th-century painter who did a series of paintings in a church dedicated to Francis of Assisi.

A Saint Salutes the Sun

SAINT FRANCIS OF ASSISI, "SONG OF BROTHER SUN," 13TH CENTURY

As a pleasure-loving youth, Francis of Assisi enjoyed poetry and songs. Later, as founder of the Franciscan monastic order, he wrote poems and hymns that celebrated the natural world as a sign of God's greatness and love. Francis, who became a saint of the Roman Catholic Church in 1228, is often shown in illustrations preaching to animals that seem to delight in his words. His "Song of Brother Sun" reveals his deep appreciation for the world around him and his belief that it reflects God's glory. Francis's poem is an outstanding example of the compassionate, joyous side of medieval piety.

Most high, omnipotent, good Lord,
Praise, glory and honor and benediction all, are Thine.
To Thee alone do they belong, most High,
And there is no man fit to mention Thee.

Praise be to Thee, my Lord, with all Thy Creatures,
Especially to my worshipful brother sun,
The which lights up the day, and through him dost Thou
  brightness give;
And beautiful is he and radiant with splendor great;
Of Thee, most High, signification gives.

Praised be my Lord, for sister moon and for the stars,
In heaven Thou has formed them clear and precious and fair.
Praised be my Lord for brother wind
And for the air and clouds and fair and every kind of weather,
By the which Thou givest to Thy creatures nourishment.
Praised be my Lord for sister water,
The which is greatly helpful and humble and precious and pure.
Praised be my Lord for brother fire,
By the which Thou lightest up the dark.
And fair is he and gay and mighty and strong.
Praised be my Lord for our sister, mother earth,

The which sustains and keeps us
And brings forth diverse fruits with grass and flowers bright.

Praised be my Lord for those who for Thy love forgive
And weakness bear and tribulation
Blessed those who shall in peace endure,
For by Thee, most High, shall they be crowned.

Praised be my Lord for our sister, the bodily death,
From the which no living man can flee.
Woe to them who die in mortal sin;

Blessed those who shall find themselves in Thy most holy will,
For the second death shall do them no ill.

Praise ye and bless ye my Lord, and give Him thanks,
And be subject unto Him with great humility.

Francis of Assisi preaches to birds, while a friendly lion and a member of the women's order founded by Clare gather around him.

text continued from page 131

Church certainly did not want women from respectable families to go out begging. So Francis's friend and follower, Clare, established an order of cloistered women, the Poor Clares. In her autobiographical *Testament,* Clare describes the principles she learned from Saint Francis: "I admonish and exhort in the Lord Jesus Christ all my Sisters . . . to . . . strive always to follow the way of holy simplicity, humility and poverty and to live worthily and holily, as we have been taught by our blessed Father Francis."

Frederick II of Germany, intelligent, curious, independent, and ambitious, is a good symbol for some of the forces that made the 12th and early 13th centuries a time of enormous excitement in Europe. It was an era of military campaigns, revolts, high-stakes political maneuvering between kings and popes, heresies and persecutions, and radical intellectual debates in the new universities that were being founded while Dominic and Francis preached. But it was also a time when many people found comfort and meaning in what they saw as a return to the virtues of early Christianity: compassion, poverty, humility, and service to others. As a beloved example of living by those virtues, Francis of Assisi is as much a representative of his age as any emperor or pope.

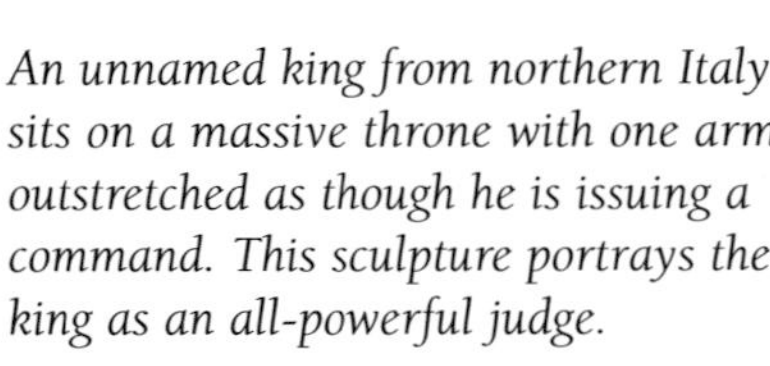

An unnamed king from northern Italy sits on a massive throne with one arm outstretched as though he is issuing a command. This sculpture portrays the king as an all-powerful judge.

CHAPTER 10

HIGH IDEALS AND LOW MANEUVERS

THE RISE OF UNIVERSITIES AND THE DECLINE OF THE PAPACY

Two influential men once dined together in Paris, one talking while the other listened eagerly. One was a scholar, the other a king. Between them they represented two important developments of the later 13th century: a passion for crusading and a passion for learning.

The king was Louis IX, later known as Saint Louis (the American city of St. Louis is named for him). Although Louis was monarch of France, he spent little of his reign there. In 1248 he left the kingdom in the capable hands of his mother, Blanche of Castile, and set off on a crusade with a small army, hoping to capture Egypt. Louis's enthusiasm got the better of him—as his ship neared its goal, Louis ignored all warnings and jumped into the sea in full armor to wade ashore with the first wave of knights.

Louis IX of France (top right) with his mother, Blanche of Castile (top left), who ruled for him when he went on several crusades. At the bottom of this illumination is an author dictating to a scribe, perhaps representing Louis's great interest in learning.

Louis survived his risky plunge only to find himself embroiled in a long struggle against the Arab forces in Egypt. However, dysentery, a serious intestinal disorder, was a greater threat to his army than war. Louis and his army were captured—a blessing in disguise for the king, who was saved from dying of dysentery by Arab doctors. Louis bought his freedom and that of his army and returned briefly to France, but crusading was his life. It was also his death. In 1270 he perished of typhoid fever in Tunisia, in North Africa, on his final crusade.

Before he died, though, Louis dined with Thomas Aquinas, a professor at the University of

"For the sire of Courtenay and Monseigneur Jean de Saillenay told me how six Turks seized the king's horse by the bridle and were going to take him prisoner, and how he, with great slashing sword cuts, delivered himself from then unaided."

—Jean de Joinville, a noble who wrote an account of crusading with King Louis IX of France, 13th century

Paris and the leading intellectual of his time. Aquinas's conversation was so enlightening and fast-flowing that the king had three scribes working at dinner to record his words. The great thinker's background was as distinguished as his intellect. Thomas Aquinas was born near Naples, Italy, in 1225 into a family related to Emperor Frederick II of Germany. The family was appalled when young Thomas decided to enter the Dominican order. His father, a count, felt that no member of his family should become a begging friar, and he offered to help the boy become a bishop if he was set on going into the Church. His mother pleaded tearfully with him and tried to kidnap him from the order. His six brothers tried to corrupt him and break his resolve by bringing a woman to his bed. Aquinas would be neither swayed nor tempted. After studying at the University of Naples, he earned a doctorate of theology at the University of Paris, where he became a highly honored teacher and scholar. Thomas Aquinas was so well regarded by his fellow Dominicans that when he died in 1274, they boiled his body to remove his bones and keep them as relics, holy objects. The church recognized him as a saint shortly after his death.

In both Naples and Paris, Aquinas was part of a world of teaching and learning that had existed for little more than a century: the world of the university. By the early 12th century, some professors such as Peter Abelard began teaching students who paid to attend their lectures. Major cities such as Paris attracted a number of these lecturers, and students flocked to listen to their debates about theology. The clusters of lecturers developed into the first universities. Students paying for the lectures wanted a certificate to show their knowledge. In the early 13th century, the universities became more structured, with set curriculums, licensed professors, and examinations.

STUDENTS BEG TO GO TO SCHOOL

Two types of universities developed. One type was the student-run professional school, such as the University of Bologna, known for the study of law. Students at these schools were in their late twenties and had clear professional goals. They wanted the university to prepare them properly for their chosen careers. They formed an association called a *universitas* that set the standards professors had to meet, including the length of lectures and the subject matter to be covered. Professors could not even leave town without the students' consent. In defense, the professors formed their own association to set requirements for the exams students had to pass to earn degrees, the qualifications for becoming a teacher, and lecture fees.

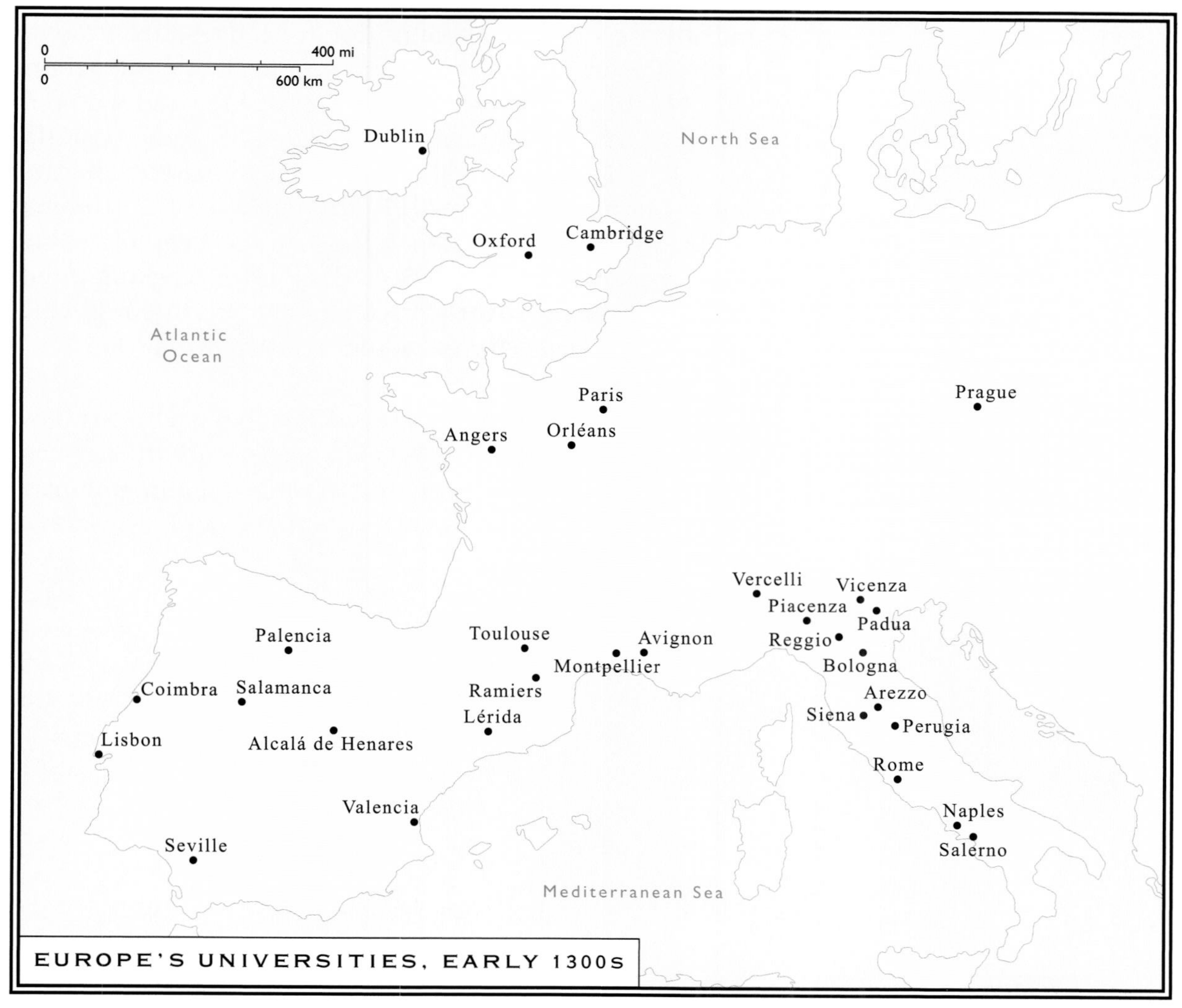

EUROPE'S UNIVERSITIES, EARLY 1300S

The professors, who were called masters in the Middle Ages, ran the second type of university. The University of Paris—run by the masters' guild, or professional association—was the model for this type. Most students at Paris were very young, usually between 13 and 18 years old. Inexperienced and away from home, many of these young men neglected their studies while pursuing the proverbial wine, women, and song. They also fought with the townspeople over such things as high rents, unpaid bills, and damage caused by the students' rowdiness.

Tension between students and townspeople led to riots, and after a particularly serious riot in 1200 resulted in some deaths, the university's masters took control of the situation. They obtained charters from the French king and the pope that guaranteed their academic freedom to study Aristotle, a Greek philosopher, and set rules for both masters and students. Masters would provide the guidance the students needed. A master had to be at least 21, have completed six years of academic work, wear a dark gown reaching to his heels, and behave soberly. Each student had to enroll with a particular master who would be responsible for both teaching and discipline.

Although some pupils studied theology (religion), law, or medicine, the majority pursued bachelor-of-arts degrees. They spent four years attending lectures in Latin grammar, logical argument, arithmetic, geometry, and astronomy.

Students listen to a professor in a classroom at the University of Bologna, which may have been the earliest university in Europe. The students ran the school, not the teachers.

"I, a wandering scholar lad,
Born for toil and sadness,
Oftentimes am driven by poverty to madness."

—Part of a student's begging song, used to solicit donations, Carmina Burana, a collection of late medieval student songs

When a student was at least 20 years old and felt ready to take his degree examination, the masters formed a committee to question him, awarding the degree if he knew the material well. Advanced degrees in law and theology took an additional five to seven years; candidates for the theology degree had to be at least 35 years old. The students took their work seriously, according to one French historian: "Almost all the students at Paris, foreigners and natives, did absolutely nothing except learn or hear something new. . . . They wrangled and disputed . . . they impudently uttered all kinds of affronts and insults against one another."

School was expensive. A student needed a patron, such as a family member or clergyman, to help pay for tuition, books, and room and board. Students also relied on alms, spending their summer vacations begging for money to support them for the next year. One master offered a solution to the twin problems of financing education and disciplining students. Around 1258 he founded a residential college in Paris, leaving money in his will to pay for separate housing where students could live, eat, and study under a master's supervision. The Sorbonne, now a part of the University of Paris, takes its name from this residential college.

Wealthy boys had private tutors to prepare them for university work, but others learned the basics in the cathedral schools. Some monks and parish priests also gave lessons. Beginning in the 15th century, private donors paid to establish grammar schools such as Eton and Harrow, both in England. For instance, a London merchant named John

Students pay rapt attention to a university lecture. This 14th-century sculpture adorns the tomb of an Italian law professor.

Carpenter started a grammar school that exists today. His will provided for the teaching and housing of boys called "Carpenter's Children." In addition to giving lessons, their master saw that they learned to shave, bathed frequently, and had clean clothes and adequate shoes.

Central to the education of schoolchildren was the belief that "to spare the rod was to spoil the child." If a boy did not know his lessons, he was beaten so that the next time he came to school he would be prepared. (The youth of one school must have enjoyed hearing that one of their masters fell into a river and drowned while gathering willow twigs to make a switch.) Children learned Latin from grammar books, used dictionaries to help them translate their everyday language into Latin, practiced their sentences and Latin grammar on wax tablets, and recited Latin passages to their teachers.

Women could not go to universities, but some did learn to read and write. Noble and city women were often literate in everyday languages, although some probably could also read official Latin documents concerning land and divorce. Wills show that women bought—and left to their daughters—religious books, romances, and manuals on courtly behavior. In the art of the period, the Virgin Mary and other women often appear holding books, while men clutch swords or symbols of church office. These images indicate how closely women were identified with reading.

Women who lived in nunneries sometimes gained knowledge of Latin and classical works and made their own scholarly or artistic contributions. A 12th-century German nun, Hildegard of Bingen, wrote musical pieces that are still sung today; she wrote essays on medicine as well. A lay woman named Jacoba Felicie practiced medicine very successfully in Paris until she got into trouble with the

University of Paris because she did not have a university degree. In her defense, a number of men and women came forward to testify that she had cured them after the doctors of the university had failed. Felicie, like many women who had practical knowledge of the human body through direct contact with patients, was better informed than the book-trained university men. Women also knew much more about healing herbs than did the doctors.

The best medical school of the 12th and 13th centuries was in Salerno, Sicily. Like Spain, Sicily was a mixture of western European, Byzantine Greek, and Muslim intellectual traditions. Medical students at Salerno studied Greek and Arabic medical texts, which were superior to those of the West. They learned anatomy by dissecting human cadavers, a practice forbidden in Paris, where students dissected pigs instead.

Queen Isabella of France holds court in her lavishly decorated bedchamber, where a well-known French author, Christine de Pisan, presents a volume of her poetry. Though women weren't allowed to attend universities, noblewomen did learn to read, and some became scholars and artists.

"Daughters of God, I advise you and I have advised you from my youth that you love one another, so that... you might be like the angels as a bright shining light strong in your powers."

—Hildegard of Bingen in a letter to her nuns, 12th century

A medical degree may have been impressive, but the most prestigious degree was in theology, or religious studies. Medieval theologians had to learn a body of knowledge that was both very old and quite new—at least to them. The works of the ancient Greek scientist and philosopher Aristotle had long been lost to western Europe, but Arab scholars had discovered his books in Persia and translated them into Arabic. The Muslims brought these works to Spain, where Jewish scholars translated them into Hebrew. Finally, Latin translations from the Hebrew reached the European universities and sparked immense excitement among scholars. The Church, however, was concerned because Aristotle's philosophy, known as logic, suggested that knowledge of God could be gained through human reason rather than by observing nature or receiving divine revelations.

A KING FOR ALL AND ALL FOR THE POPE

The challenge was to make the logic of Aristotle and other ancient scholars compatible with Christianity. Abelard and other 12th-century thinkers had used reason to understand questions of faith. Thomas Aquinas not only studied the problem raised for Christians by Aristotle's works but made an extremely important contribution to it with his book *Summa Theologica*, meaning the highest or most important theology. In his *Summa Theologica*, Aquinas applied Aristotle's logic to all aspects of Christian teaching.

Aquinas argued that "the existence of truth is self-evident. For whoever denies the existence of truth grants that truth does not exist: and, if truth does not exist, then the proposition 'Truth does not exist' is true: and if there is anything true, there must be truth." Aquinas concluded that the knowledge revealed in the Bible and the truth reached by Aristotle's logic must agree, because truth is truth—a person could not believe one thing on faith and something else on reason. But Aquinas also said that some concepts could not be understood by human reason. Only God's reason, which was also infinite, could understand them. Humans would have to be guided by faith in matters that were beyond the limits of their reason.

Part of the *Summa Theologica* deals with Aquinas's theory of natural law—the principles that explain how the natural world works. Natural law, Aquinas believed, stems from God's perfect order, but humans can understand by observing the world around us.

According to Aquinas, natural law relies on human reason to establish moral laws in society. Aquinas found proof for his theory in the ability of human beings to distinguish between good and evil and to live good lives. Part of the *Summa Theologica* is about governing human society for the good of the whole community, not just the individual. A king, for example, should not act to preserve and advance himself at the expense of his subjects; instead, he should promote good for all. To help people survive and work together for good, a society needs rules about such things as marriage, educating children, and living in a community.

Aquinas was very much a man of his times. By the 13th century, Europe had begun to redefine shared rights and responsibilities in political life, through documents such as the Magna Carta and representative assemblies such as the English Parliament and local governing bodies in other countries. These assemblies were weak and could not direct the kings, but they did represent the idea that the king should work for the good of his realm as a whole.

By the end of the 13th century the monarchs of Europe and the

text continues on page 146

In these illustrations from a medieval medical textbook, a surgeon demonstrates how to remove an arrow and a lance (middle left) and cut open the chest and stomach (middle right). At the bottom, he identifies injured intestines and an abscess.

A Merchant's Adventures in Central Asia

MARCO POLO, TRAVELS, 1298

In 1271 a Venetian merchant named Marco Polo accompanied his father and his uncle on a trip to China. They spent 20 years traveling through India, Southeast Asia, and China under the patronage of the Chinese emperor Kublai Khan. After he returned to Italy in 1292, Marco Polo was captured in battle and imprisoned in Genoa. In prison, he met the romance writer Rustichello of Pisa who helped him write a memoir of his travels. His book recounts the dangers they encountered along the route and the customs learned along the way.

I have much to tell you about the Tartars [a Turkish-speaking people of the central Asian steppes]. They spend the winter in steppes and warm regions where there is good grazing and pasturage for their beasts. In summer they live in cool regions, among mountains and valleys, where they find water and woodland as well as pasturage. . . . They have circular houses made of wood and covered with felt, which they carry about with them on four-wheeled wagons wherever they go. For the framework of rods is so neatly and skillfully constructed that it is light to carry. And every time they unfold their house and set it up, the door is always facing south.

They also have excellent two-wheeled carts covered with black felt, of such good design that if it rained all the time the rain would never wet anything in the cart. These are drawn by oxen and camels. And in these carts they carry their wives and children and all they need in the way of utensils. And I assure you that the womenfolk buy and sell and do all that is needful for their husbands and households. For the men do not bother themselves about anything but hunting and warfare and falconry. They live on meat and milk and game and on Pharaoh's rats, which are abundant everywhere in the steppes. They have no objection to eating the flesh of horses and dogs and drinking mares' milk. In fact they eat flesh of any sort. Not for anything in the world would one of them touch another's wife; they are too well assured that such a deed is wrongful and disgraceful. The wives are true and loyal to their husbands and very good at their household tasks. Even if there are as many as ten or twenty of them in one household, they live together in concord and unity beyond praise, so that you would never hear a harsh world spoken. They all devote themselves to their various tasks and the care of the children, who are held among them in common.

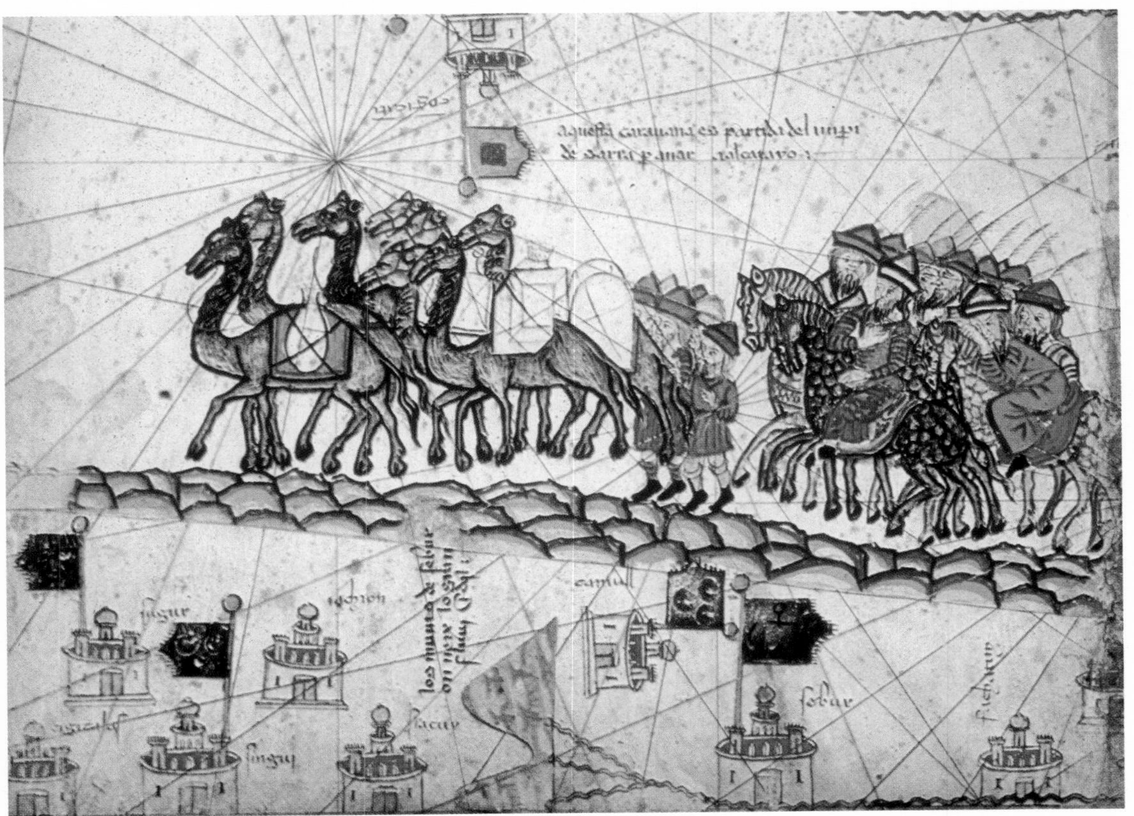

Merchants ride behind camels loaded with goods—silks, rugs, spices, and precious gems—on the caravan route across Asia known as the Great Silk Road. This is the route Marco Polo took to China.

Thomas Aquinas was a theologian and philosopher whose writings are still studied today. He used the logic of Aristotle to prove the existence of God and support the teachings of the church. He was made a saint soon after his death.

text continued from page 143

popes were again in conflict. Philip IV of France was less idealistic than his crusading grandfather, the Saint Louis who had listened so eagerly to Thomas Aquinas over dinner. Pitting himself against Edward I of England, Philip skirmished over the possessions England still held in France. For both Edward and Philip, fighting required money. The English people had become increasingly used to taxation, but the French monarch had to look elsewhere for funds.

Philip identified two sources of wealth to tap: the Jews and the clergy. In 1306 Philip expelled the Jews from France—but seized their wealth before they left. (Edward had already plundered and expelled the English Jews in 1292.) While there had been local persecutions of Jews throughout the Middle Ages, the monarchs had protected them before. The Jews now fled to eastern Europe, Russia, Italy, the new Christian kingdoms of Spain, and Granada, the last remaining Muslim kingdom in Spain.

Philip was aided in his schemes by a new class of university-trained lawyers. William de Nogaret, Philip's chief adviser, had studied the most practical subjects at university, including the law. His rise to power was based on his good education, boldness, and loyalty to his monarch. One of Nogaret's successes was helping the king get his hands on some church funds. Those funds came from lay people, or ordinary folk, who paid money to the clergy every year. The clergy sent part of the money to the pope in Rome. Philip wanted to halt the flow of money from his kingdom.

The papacy had already lost some of its prestige through its involvement in political disputes and battles throughout the 12th century. The College of Cardinals tried to repair the loss of spiritual leadership by choosing a pious Italian monk as pope. The cardinals expected Pope Celestine V to be a spiritual figurehead while they continued their political and financial maneuverings. But the more Celestine learned about their corruption, the more worried he became. Celestine began to have dreams in which he heard a voice saying that it was the will of God that he resign. In a matter of months, Celestine did just that, fearing for the salvation of his soul. It was an extraordinary event—no pope had ever resigned before. He was succeeded by Pope Boniface VIII in 1294. Boniface's critics later suggested that Boniface had rigged a tube into Celestine's chamber and spoken "God's" words himself.

Once in power, Boniface issued a rule to decide once and for all who was the most powerful, the emperor or the pope. He declared that the pope was the absolute head of all Christians: "Of this one and only Church there is one body and one head—not two heads, like a monster." He also issued a rule to stop kings and other heads of state from taxing the clergy. Philip was insulted by this attempt to restrict what he considered to be his right. King Philip's lawyer Nogaret plotted with some of the pope's enemies from Rome to capture Boniface at his vacation home. They hoped he would change his mind about his ruling. He did not, though. Since a captive pope was just an embarrassment, they released him. Boniface died a month later. The prestige of the papacy had sunk so low that no one retaliated against Philip for the attack. Later the cardinals elected a French-speaking pope who, fearing Roman mobs, settled in the city of Avignon in present-day France. His successors stayed there during a period called the Avignon papacy.

The 13th century produced dedicated rulers, well-educated professional government employees, and a master theologian. But by the end of the century, the crusading spirit that had inspired King Louis IX still had not recaptured the Holy Land from the Muslims, and England and France were on the verge of war. Things looked bad—and although no one knew it yet, they would soon get worse. In the century ahead, the papacy reached its lowest point, and the people of Europe suffered unimaginable devastation.

Pope Boniface VIII quarreled with both Edward I of England and Philip IV of France because he wanted to stop them from taxing the clergy. He died a month after agents of Philip IV captured him.

CHAPTER 11

MATTERS OF LIFE AND DEATH

FAMINE, PLAGUE, AND WAR

Francesco de Marco Datini of the northern Italian city of Prato lived through the worst and the best of the Middle Ages. He was only a child when one of the worst disasters in history, the plague outbreak called the Black Death, raged through Italy in 1348. The plague killed Francesco's parents—along with about a third of the population of Europe. But the plague was only one of many calamities that struck during the 14th century.

Even before Francesco's birth, many Europeans were struggling to survive in a world made harsher by population growth and climate change. The population of Europe rose steadily from around 1050 to the early 14th century. By the late 13th century, the population had outgrown the land's capacity to feed the people. Years of farming had stripped the soil of the nutrients plants needed to grow. Peasants in the hills of Italy, England, Spain, and France farmed infertile soils that yielded barely enough food for

In 1300, the average European peasant lived for only 25 years. Peasants worked hard every day except Sunday in all kinds of weather, and their diet was poor. During the Great Famine in the early 14th century, many of the poor throughout Europe starved to death.

them. Many did not survive. About 30 percent of infants died, and for poor peasants and city dwellers infant mortality was even higher—as many as half of their children died before reaching the age of three.

With food already scarce, a long-lasting shift in climate made things much worse in northern Europe in the first quarter of the 14th century. It rained so much in the summer of 1315 that wet weather ruined the crops. The rain continued, making the fields too muddy for planting winter wheat in the fall and summer crops in the following spring. The harvest of 1316 was pitiful; the grain that could be harvested was so damp it had to be dried in ovens. The rain continued into 1317. Cattle died of diseases brought on by the wet weather and lack of grain. People perished, too. During the Great Famine, which lasted from 1315 to 1317, and again in the early 1320s, starvation devastated the poor. They died in country lanes and city alleys. An English monk reported that, "Four pennies worth of coarse bread was not enough to feed a common man for one day. The usual kinds of meat, suitable for eating, were too scarce; horse meat was precious; plump dogs were stolen."

Starving people committed desperate acts. Prisoners tore apart and ate new inmates who were put into their jail cells. When a charity tried to help the starving in London, 60 men, women, and children were crushed to death as the crowd pushed forward to get the pennies that were being given away to buy food. The monasteries, which usually gave food to the poor, could not help because their crops were ruined, too. Grain was heavy to transport, so bringing large quantities of it from southern Europe, which did not experience the same bad weather, was impractical. The king of England tried to do it anyway, but pirates boarded the grain ships before they reached port, stole the cargo, and sold it at a huge profit.

In agricultural societies that depend on locally produced food, famines are always a danger and a dread. Most rich people can find enough to eat; it is the poor who die in famines. Disease, however, can attack any social class, as Europeans learned to their horror in the mid-14th century.

RATUS RATUS STRIKES AGAIN

The bubonic plague, a deadly and very contagious disease, had not struck Europe since the reign of the Byzantine emperor Justinian in the sixth century. The 14th century, however, brought an outbreak of plague so widespread and severe that daily life was devastated not just in Europe but in China and the Arab world as well. Modern scientists still debate the exact nature of this plague, but they know that it

In this artist's fanciful depiction of the plague, Saint Sebastian (top) hears the prayers of urban dwellers. Meanwhile, priests administer the last rites to the plague-stricken corpses, but others, such as the man in the foreground, dies in the act of burial.

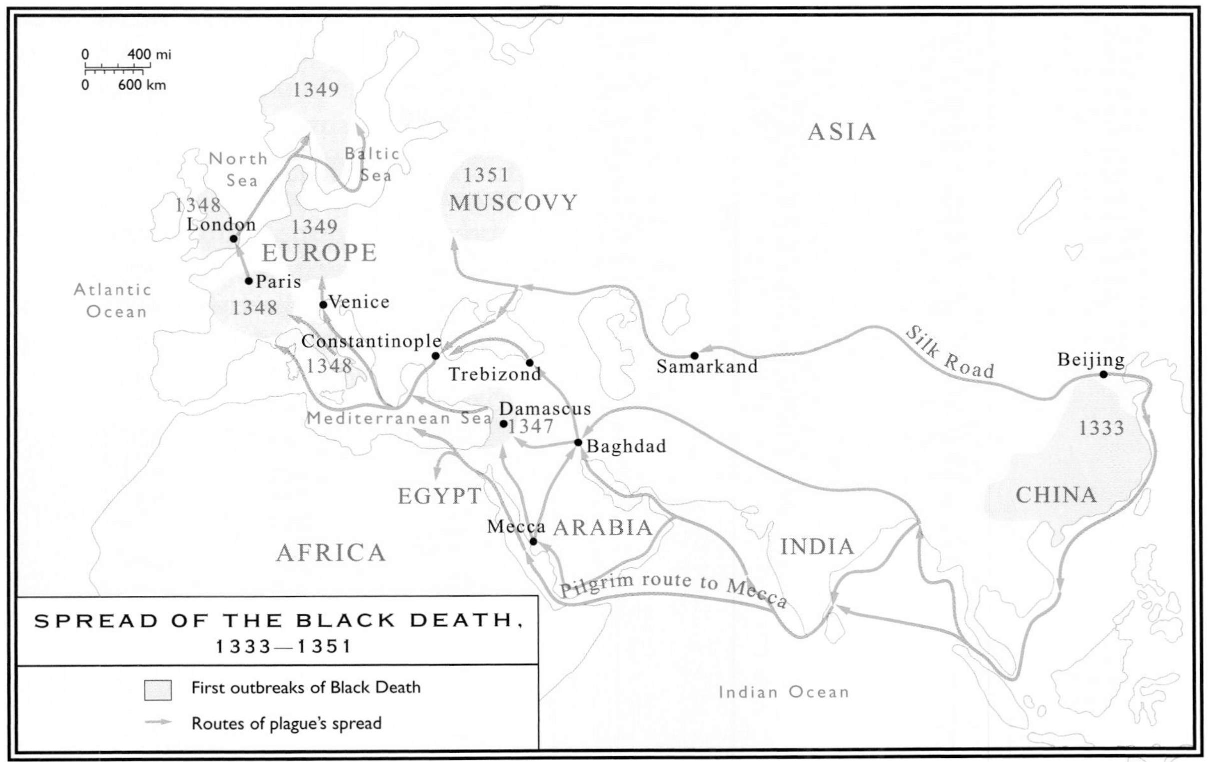

originated in Central Asia and was transmitted to humans by fleas that lived on infected rats. Fleas thrived on the common European house rat (*Ratus ratus* in Latin), which lived wherever people did. When infected fleas bit people, as often happened, the disease spread to human victims.

The plague came to Europe from Asia, carried by traders. Its path can be traced along the Silk Road, the route followed by caravans bringing silk and spices from eastern Asia across the steppes, or plains, of central Asia. Caravan traders carried not just goods but also grain to feed their animals, and where there was grain, there were rats. China and Mongolia were infected first—an Arab writer who died of the plague wrote that it raged in eastern Asia in the early 1330s. The plague struck India, then Persia.

Meanwhile, cargoes containing infected rats and fleas arrived at trading ports on the Black Sea. One such a cargo was loaded onto a boat that set sail for Venice, Italy, in 1347.

"The Just Wrath of God"

GIOVANNI BOCCACCIO, THE DECAMERON, 1353

One of the most vivid descriptions of the plague occurs in The Decameron, *a collection of stories by the Italian poet Giovanni Boccaccio, who witnessed the outbreak of the disease. The book tells of a fictional group of Italian merchants and nobles who gather in a castle to avoid contagion and entertain each other by telling stories. The book, Boccaccio's masterpiece, begins with an account of the Black Death that is ravaging the proud city of Florence. Boccaccio mentions one of the explanations that Europeans offered for the dreadful disease—that it was God's punishment for their sins.*

The mortal pestilence then arrive[d] in the excellent city of Florence, which surpasses every other Italian city in nobility. Whether through the operations of the heavenly bodies, or sent upon us mortals through our wicked deeds by the just wrath of God for our correction, the plague had begun some years before in Eastern countries. . . . It did not work as it had in the East, where anyone who bled from the nose had a manifest sign of inevitable death. But in its early stages both men, and women too, acquired certain swellings, either in the groin or under the armpits. The swellings reached the size of a common apple and others were as big as an egg, some more or less. . . . Then the appearance of the disease began to change into black or livid blotches, which showed up in many on the arms or thighs and in every other part of the body. . . . The evil was still greater than this. Not only conversation and contact with the sick carried the illness to the healthy and was cause of their common death, but even to handle the clothing or other things touched or used by the sick seemed to carry with it that same disease. . . .

Such events and many others similar to them . . . conjure up in those who remain healthy diverse fears and imaginings. . . . Almost all were inclined to a very cruel purpose, that is, to shun and to flee the sick and their belongings. . . . Others were of a contrary opinion. They affirmed that heavy drinking and enjoyment, making the rounds with singing and good cheer, the satisfaction of the appetite with everything one could, and the laughing and joking which derived from this, were the most effective for this great evil.

The sailors and merchants aboard the ship were dying of a terrible disease, so Venice refused them permission to land. But the vessel docked at other Italian ports, unloading rats and fleas along with cargo. The disease spread rapidly through Italy and then along trade routes until it had infected most of Europe, both city and country. But the pattern of the disease was odd. Some villages were decimated, whereas others had no sickness. This devastating outbreak of plague skipped entirely over a few regions, including Poland.

The plague took three forms. The Italian poet Giovanni Boccaccio, who did not catch the disease but saw it in action, described some of its symptoms: "it betrayed itself by the emergence of certain tumors in the groin or the armpits, some of which grew as large as a common apple, others as an egg, some more, some less." One form of the disease caused buboes, or swellings of the lymph nodes and made a person's blood collect and congeal under the skin, leaving black patches. The symptoms of this form gave the disease its two names—bubonic plague and the Black Death. Another form of the plague resembled pneumonia, while another infected the blood, causing instant death.

The plague's effects were enormous. Unlike famine, the disease claimed victims of every social class. Rats—and their fleas—lived in the thatched roofs of peasants' huts, in the dirty ditches and streets of cities, and in the moats and

Death carries off a victim in triumph in this 15th-century image representing the horror of the plagues that swept through Europe and killed nearly half its population.

wells of castles and palaces. Some cities, such as Florence and London, lost half their population. Perhaps a third of Europe's population died in the first wave of plague. The number of dead was so great that normal ceremonies of death, for Christian and Muslim alike, were often set aside, and the bodies were buried in mass graves. Priests tried to help the dying by giving them their last rites; as a result, priests had the highest death rate. Doctors offered various cures, all ineffective. Very few sick people recovered.

No one knew what caused the plague. Some Arab and Christian writers thought it came from air that was heavy and polluted. Others believed it was the result of generally sinful living and that only prayer and self-punishment would help. Some prejudiced Christians said Jews had poisoned the wells, leading to new laws that required Jews to wear a distinctive mark on their clothing so that they could be watched. Still others, concluding that the plague spread through contact with the sick, isolated themselves in the hope of escaping infection. People fled from plague-struck locations to the

A man who has contracted the plague is carried in his bed from the Italian city of Sansepolero. The plague returned to Europe about every 20 years during the 1300s. People began to suspect that the disease was contagious, so they removed the victims from the city.

countryside or to uninfected cities, but soon those cities began to deny entrance to people from infected areas.

The plague devastated Egypt and other regions of the Arab world as well as Europe. An Arab historian named Ibn Khaldun wrote, "Civilization both in the East and the West was visited by a destructive plague which devastated nations and caused populations to vanish. It swallowed up many of the good things of civilization and wiped them out." His comments were based on the first outbreak of 1347–49, but that nightmare was not the end of the plague. It returned about every 20 years throughout the Middle Ages and for some time afterward. Although the plague's effects were never again as sweeping as the first wave, the later outbreaks brought death to many people and affected the lives of the survivors, including Francesco de Marco Datini.

After the deaths of his parents in the first plague outbreak, Datini was lucky. He had a small inheritance and was raised by a woman whom he regarded affectionately as a mother. At a young age, Datini apprenticed himself to a merchant in Florence so that he could learn to trade. Becoming an apprentice made sense for Datini as a way to earn a living.

TINKER, TAILOR, PEASANT, REBEL

Apprenticeship was part of a system that allowed craftsmen and merchants to regulate their trades. Like university masters, craftsmen and merchants in cities created guilds to keep untrained, unlicensed practitioners from entering their businesses. Masters of each craft or trade set standards of quality for basic products. A youth who wanted to be a master had to meet those standards. A baker or a shoemaker, for instance, had to prove to his guild that he could produce a fine-quality loaf of wheat bread or a sturdy shoe. Only after having done so could he become a master of his trade and open shop. Makers of poor-quality wares were punished; if a baker sold bread with sawdust in it, the guild fined him and paraded him through the streets with the loaf around his neck. Guilds of merchants who dealt in banking and long-

Merchants work in their shops in a French town. From left to right are tailors, furriers, a barber, and a grocer. In the late Middle Ages towns grew, and laborers became more organized.

distance trade, like the guild Datini joined, fined their members for fraud. The guild system made it harder for someone to enter a craft or trade, but it gave consumers confidence in the goods and services they bought.

Masters trained apprentices in their trades. An apprentice's family or friends agreed to pay a master a sum of money to train the youth for an agreed number of years, usually seven to ten, starting when the young man was about 14. The master had to provide clothing, somewhere to sleep, food, and training and, when the apprentice became more skilled at the work, the master paid him a small salary. The apprentice swore not to spend the master's money on gambling or the theater. He could not marry, and he lived in the house of the master and his family. According to the contract for a London tailor's apprentice, the master was to "find his apprentice all necessaries, food, clothing, shoes, and bed and to teach him his craft in all its particulars." The apprentice, in return, was "to keep his master's secrets, to do him no injury and commit no excessive waste of his goods. He is not to play at dice... or checkers or any other unlawful games but is to conduct himself soberly, justly, piously, well, and honorably, and to be a faithful and good servant." Relationships between masters and apprentices varied considerably. Some were close and friendly, others abusive. One English apprentice complained to the local court that his master had "come at 11 or 12 o'clock at night, dragged him from his bed, and beaten him." Datini's apprenticeship took him away from his native Prato. Soon after his 15th birthday, he joined his master and other merchants who were going to Avignon, a city in southern

France that had become rich as the new seat of the papacy. Datini became a master merchant, went into business there, and prospered, importing Italian art and luxury items for the cardinals and other wealthy residents. Years later, when he was more than 40, Datini returned to Prato and married a young woman named Margherita. Although he traveled often, he and Margherita exchanged letters weekly; these letters and many others are still preserved in Datini's house in Prato.

Despite his wealth and success, Datini shared the anxieties of many people in the late Middle Ages about the plague. In 1400, during one of the recurrent outbreaks, the disease struck Prato. Datini fled with his family, heading for Bologna by mule. The danger was very real—in a letter from Florence, one of Datini's friends wrote, "I have seen two of my children die in my arms in a few hours." But Datini was more fortunate. He lived for another 10 years and died peacefully in Prato.

Guilds were not the only new form of social organization to emerge in the 13th and 14th centuries. By that time, peasant villages were forming community governments to deal with the tensions that existed at all levels of village life, such as arguments about who deserved charity or how to deal with local annoyances. Villagers passed bylaws to regulate problems and fine offenders, including people who took

Merchants belonged to guilds, which regulated the quality of the goods and produce they sold. Here, (from left to right) a sugar seller completes a sale, a merchant sells swiss chard, and a butcher does a brisk business.

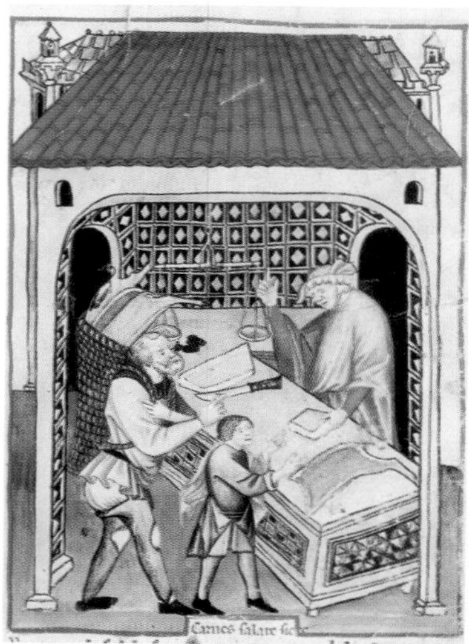

village charity when they could afford to feed themselves and those who were aggressive toward their neighbors.

The villagers administered these bylaws through the manorial court, which was run by the lord of the manor's official. Two men who argued about a debt, for example, could bring the dispute to the court and ask a jury of their neighbors to decide who was at fault. Peasants learned to argue in courts and to understand the value of written records. Cooperating in village government prepared them for a larger political arena. The plague catapulted them into that arena, especially in England.

The Black Death greatly reduced the English workforce, making labor more scarce and therefore more valuable. Peasants realized that they could demand higher wages and refuse the heavy work burdens their lords imposed. The king and nobles, recognizing the costs of giving in to peasants' demands, tried to pass laws that froze the prices of labor and products at the level of 1347, before the plague.

The king's attempt to control wages and prices failed. Peasants simply left their manors and sought higher wages elsewhere; craftsmen charged whatever customers would pay. But the royal action stirred resentment among peasants and townsfolk. They also resented being taxed to pay for England's war with France. The skirmishes between Philip IV and Edward III had developed into a full-fledged war in the 1340s called the Hundred Years War. These resentments flared up in 1381, when the royal tax collectors arrived in Essex, a county north of London. A group of peasants killed the tax collectors, igniting a revolt that spread rapidly throughout England. They were egged on by their priests, one of whom proclaimed, "The righteous poor will stand up against the cruel rich at the Day of Judgment." Said another, "Matters cannot go well in England until all things shall be held in common; when there shall be neither vassals nor lords, when the lords shall be no more masters than ourselves."

Many peasants converged on London, where craftsmen in the city joined their revolt. They killed the king's advisers and demanded a meeting with King Richard II, a boy of 15. Richard agreed to meet with the rebels' spokesmen.

"The [peasants] had as their counselor a chaplain of evil disposition named Sir John Ball, who advised them to get rid of all the lords, and of archbishops and bishops... saying that their possessions should be distributed among the laity."

—An unknown monk from York, England, describing the 1381 English Peasants' Revolt in his chronicle, late 14th century

Wat Tyler, the leader of a peasant rebellion in Essex, England, crouches at sword point before being killed. King Richard II, who was 15 years old at the time, lured Tyler to his death by agreeing to meet the rebel. After Tyler's murder, the young king stepped forward and said to the peasants, "Your leader is dead. Follow me; I am your leader."

Leading them outside the walls of London, he listened to their demands for an end to serfdom. Then one of the king's followers drew a sword and killed the rebel leader. The situation could have exploded, but Richard had the presence of mind to ride boldly forward and remind the rebels that he was their leader. He promised them freedom if they would return to their homes; later he sent out royal justices to round up the ringleaders, whom he hanged.

The Revolt of 1381 had little real effect on English serfdom, which was already declining, in part because of the labor shortage caused by the plague. Peasants continued to pay rent for the land they cultivated, but they no longer paid fees when their daughters married or their sons left the manor, and they no longer worked on the lord's property. The fines and burdens of serf status were ignored. But England was not the only place to see a peasant uprising—outbursts against the serf system occurred throughout Europe. In some places, including Spain and Poland, the result was very different for the peasants from that in England. Fearing a loss of labor, lords made rules that tied the peasants even more closely to their manors. In these places, serfdom became more binding than it had been before the plague.

The mythical figures called the Four Horsemen of the Apocalypse, Famine, Plague, War, and Death, from a 12th-century manuscript. One rider has a set of scales, two hold swords, and another has a bow and arrow. A demon waves its arms. These images represented the disasters that rocked the medieval world.

Europeans of the 14th and 15th centuries often referred to the Four Horsemen of the Apocalypse, mythical figures of dread who rode across the land spreading disaster. Both Hebrew and Christian texts refer to the Apocalypse, or end of the world. The Christian text appears in the New Testament's Book of Revelation. The first horseman was Famine; in the early 14th century, northern Europe became sadly familiar with him. The second horseman was Disease, the Black Death and later plagues. The third horseman, War, took on a new and more deadly form in the late 14th and 15th centuries.

Before that time, battles took place on battlefields and did little harm to local civilians. But during the Hundred Years' War between England and France (1337–1453), formal battles were infrequent. It was a war in which civilians became victims. France preyed on English shipping and invaded England's southern coast. English troops pillaged the French countryside, destroying vineyards and plundering livestock, crops, and valuables. War had never seemed closer or more deadly to most common folk.

As for the fourth horseman, some called him Death, and others called him Salvation. Either way, his arrival meant the end of all life on Earth. Christ would come again and collect the souls of the good, while the bad souls would be sent to Hell. Salvation seemed uncertain in those troubled years. The papacy's continual search for new sources of money dismayed people, some of whom now questioned the pope's authority. People began to turn to preachers who attacked the established church. With so many disturbing changes and so much going wrong, is it any wonder that people thought the end of the world was near?

CHAPTER 12

THE END OF THE OLD AND THE BEGINNING OF THE NEW

THE MIDDLE AGES GIVES WAY TO THE RENAISSANCE

Edward III of England was, in many ways, the ideal medieval king. He was a tall, handsome 18-year-old when he became king in 1327. A brave knight, he sometimes entered tournaments in disguise. Edward identified himself with the mythical King Arthur and founded a chivalric group of nobles like the legendary Knights of Round Table. He married a beautiful foreign princess and had many children. But, like other medieval kings, Edward was hungry for more territory to control, and he was willing to start a war to get it.

It was Edward who plunged England and France into the Hundred Years War. The immediate cause of war was that King Philip IV of France had died without leaving an heir to his throne. Edward III, who was Philip's grandson, claimed it. The French refused to have a king who descended through the female line. This excluded Edward, whose mother was a French princess. Edward wouldn't accept this; he declared himself king of France as well as England.

Edward II marries Isabelle of France in 1308. Isabelle's blue tent is decorated with the fleur-de-lis, the emblem of France, and Edward's red one is covered with lions, the symbol of England. The artist has portrayed the knights on bended knees as much shorter than the nobles in the wedding party, perhaps as a way to indicate their lesser importance.

All along, of course, Edward wanted to get his hands on Normandy and other French territory that John Lackland had lost a few generations earlier. But there were also disputes over trade. French pirates stopped English ships from taking wine from Aquitaine to England. Meanwhile, England refused to ship wool to Flanders, a French territory and one of the wealthiest cloth-manufacturing centers of Europe. In order to gain access to the raw materials they needed for their business, the weavers of Flanders sided with Edward and revolted against France.

In 1345 Edward landed an army in Normandy. The French king met him at Crécy in northern France with a mounted force twice as large. Fired up with enthusiasm, the French attacked without resting or waiting for their foot soldiers to arrive. Edward, however, had the better position, a hilltop. He also had archers armed with longbows. According to a 14th-century French chronicle, "the air began to . . . clear, and the sun to shine fair and bright, which was right in the Frenchmen's eyes and on the Englishmen's backs . . . the English archers stepped forth one pace and let fly their arrows." The French knights had to charge uphill against a shower of arrows that shot the horses out from under them. Edward won the battle, but all he had really captured was the port city of Calais.

Edward III's son, Edward the Black Prince, lands with the English army in France, to launch the second major campaign in the Hundred Years' War. The banners on the ships combine the symbols of France and England, Edward's way of saying that both countries belonged to him.

After a truce that was called during the first great outbreak of bubonic plague in the late 1340s, England launched another campaign in 1356. The Battle of Poitiers unfolded much like that of Crécy. Again the French suffered major losses. Among those captured on the battlefield was the French king John, who had been chosen to rule by the French. John spent the rest of his life in a comfortable prison in England, while his son and heir to the throne resisted, paying a ransom for his father's return.

The French suffered a defeat at the Battle of Poitiers. English foot soldiers attacked the French knights with longbows, shooting their horses out from under them and creating havoc on the field.

JOAN OF ARC TO THE RESCUE

The battles fought at Crécy and Poitiers didn't win the war, but they marked a change in the nature of warfare. They showed that battles in the field between armored, mounted knights with swords and lances were obsolete. The soldier of the future was a foot soldier or infantryman armed with a longbow, crossbow, or pike. The longbow, accurate and easily reloaded, could rain volleys of arrows. The crossbow was powerful enough to penetrate chain mail, flexible armor made of interlocking metal rings. Armor had to be redesigned with curved surfaces to deflect the crossbow's arrows. A pike had a long shaft, a blade like an ax, and a sharp point. It could be used to pull a knight off his horse, spear him or his horse from underneath, chop at a foe on the ground, or form a barricade to halt a cavalry charge.

Foot soldiers came from both the peasantry and the lower ranks of townsmen. Many were violent criminals or impatient youths who wanted to make quick fortunes and

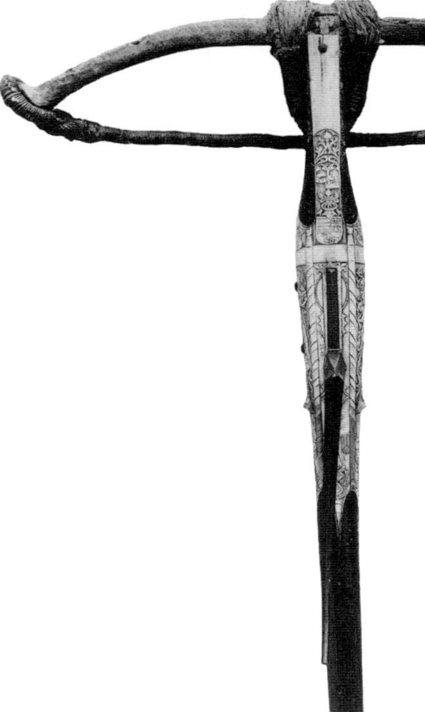

It took great skill and strength to handle medieval weapons. The crossbow was used to send a steel-tipped bolt into enemy ranks and could even penetrate armor. The flail, a steel ball on a chain attached to a shaft, was used to bash people.

preferred the excitement of fighting to the work of an apprentice or plowman. They were mercenaries—soldiers paid to fight—and when the pay ran out, their commanders let them pillage the countryside. These marauding mercenary armies devastated France.

A new round of fighting broke out in the early 15th century. The French king Charles VI, sick and suffering from memory loss, could not control his quarreling nobles. King Henry V of England seized the chance to invade the troubled country. The French had not learned the military lessons of the previous century. At the Battle of Agincourt in northern France in 1415, French knights once again charged on their horses into bowmen and pike men. This time they charged downhill into mud and got stuck. Henry made a treaty with the French and married the daughter of the king of France; by treaty, their son would rule both countries. The treaty also declared that Prince Charles, Henry's new wife's brother and the heir to the French throne, was of illegitimate birth and so couldn't become king.

Charles, a weak-willed young man, accepted the treaty, but a young peasant girl named Joan of Arc is credited with giving him the courage to act like a king. After Burgundians, from an independent province of the German Empire, had looted Joan's peaceful village, she had visions that urged her to make an appeal to Charles to rescue France from the Burgundians and the English. According to a later transcript, Joan "declared that at the age of 13 she had a voice from God to help her and guide her. And for the first time she was much afraid. And this voice came towards noon, in summer, in her father's garden." She persuaded one of the prince's captains that her visions were real and that she was serious about seeing the prince, and he gave her a suit of armor and an escort to Charles. Dressed as a knight, she went to see the prince. So low were his fortunes that he was willing to listen to this strange girl who claimed to have heard the voices of saints telling her to rescue France.

Charles followed her guidance, allowed her to go with the army, and the course of the war changed. After Joan rescued

The young villager Joan of Arc meets with Charles VII, who allowed her to join the fight against the English and Burgundians at first, but betrayed her in the end. In this painting she wears a dress and her hair hangs long. However, some historical accounts say that she cut off her hair and disguised herself as a knight to march with the French army into battle.

an important French city from an English siege, Charles was officially crowned king of France. Joan was less fortunate. In 1431 the English captured her and put her on trial in Rouen, a city in northern France, for witchcraft and heresy. At her trial she demonstrated bravery and devotion to God, declaring to the bishop who prosecuted her, "You say that you are my judge; consider well what you do; for in truth I am sent from God, and you are putting yourself in great peril." The bishop was not swayed, and Joan was found guilty and burned at the stake in a public square. King Charles, to his shame, made no attempt to rescue the woman who had won him his throne, but she immediately became the symbol of resistance for France. The French kept on fighting to drive out the English, and by 1453 the Hundred Years War was finally over. The English had started the war to regain their former Angevin Empire in France, but in the end they held only the city of Calais, the same city that Edward III won in the first battle of the long war.

By that time, England was torn by a long civil war between two branches of the royal family, the Yorkists and the Lancastrians. One of the most notable Yorkists to hold the throne was King Richard III, although his two young nephews had a better claim to it. When they disappeared

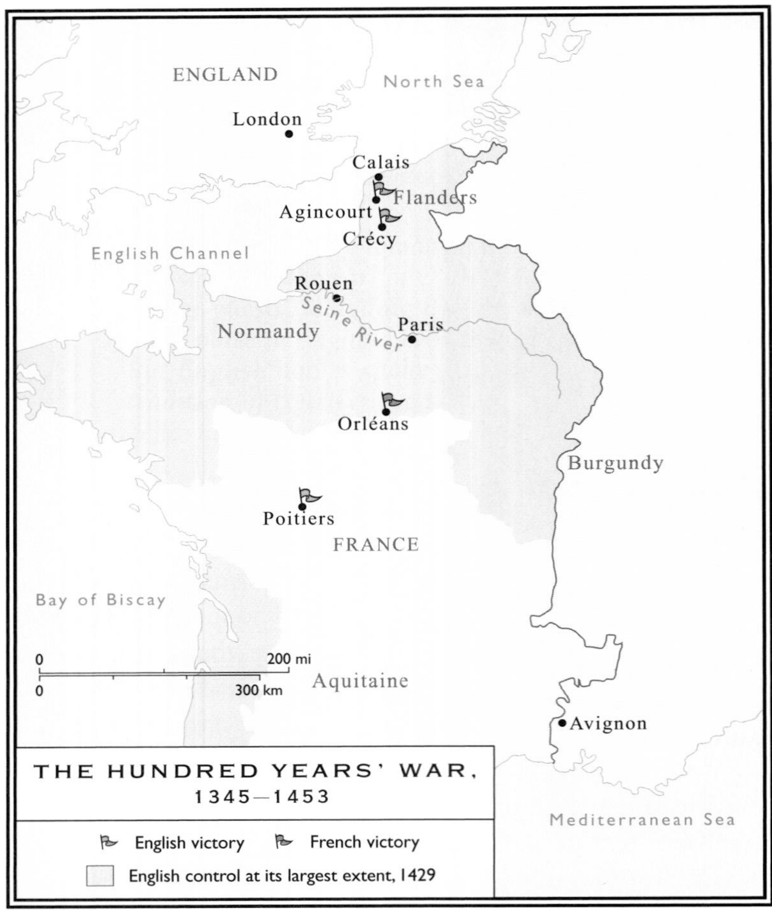

THE HUNDRED YEARS' WAR, 1345–1453

into the Tower of London, built first by William the Conqueror, Richard was accused of having them murdered; their fate remains a mystery. The civil war ended in 1485, when Henry Tudor, a Lancastrian, defeated Richard at the Battle of Bosworth Field and made himself King Henry VII, founder of the Tudor dynasty.

At the end of the 15th century, many systems of government and political situations existed across Europe. England was a monarchy with a parliament and a king who was subject to law. France was a monarchy in which the king had almost unlimited power. Both Italy and Germany consisted of independent cities and fiefdoms, each with its own ruler. Portugal was monarchy with an interest in seafaring; its sailors were busy exploring the west coast of Africa. And in Spain, the kingdoms of Aragon and Castile were involved in an ongoing civil war.

MONEY MAKES THE CHURCH LOSE GROUND

In Castile, a princess named Isabella vied with her half-brother for the throne. She looked for a marriage alliance that would help her win it, and in 1469 she married Ferdinand, a prince of Aragon who was also struggling to secure his throne. Shrewd and unscrupulous, they made an effective pair—within a decade, both were in power. After crushing the opposition in their own kingdoms, they turned their attention to Granada, the last Muslim state in Spain. They conquered it in 1492, bringing the long *Reconquista* to its end.

War was expensive, and the king and queen had borrowed heavily to pay for it. They needed money, and one solution was to expel the Jews and seize their property. The exceedingly pious Isabella also wanted to make Spain a Catholic country. The expulsion of Jews was a step in that direction. With the support of the pope, she and Ferdinand began to hold trials, called inquisitions, to investigate and try people accused of heresy as well as converted Jews and Muslims. The converts were assumed to have adopted Catholicism to save their lives and property rather than from true conviction.

The Spanish Inquisition became notorious because torture, which was allowed under papal rules, was used to question the accused. The persecution and burning of Muslim converts began in Seville in 1481, wiping out Arabs who had long been Christian. Next came Jews, who were hunted down and either killed or driven out of the country. The Inquisition achieved Isabella's goal of making Spain almost entirely Catholic. Wealth confiscated from victims of the Inquisition paid for the war with Granada and also

The wedding party celebrating the marriage of Duke Philip the Good of Burgundy to Isabel of Portugal in 1430 was an elegant affair. The Burgundians, from the eastern region of France, were politically powerful and set the style for the aristocrats of the 15th century.

Santa Maria la Blanca, in Toledo, Spain, was originally built as a synagogue. It was turned into a church around 1550. Many Jews, along with Muslims, were killed or driven out of Spain during the Inquisition.

helped pay for new ventures such as the voyages of Christopher Columbus, which Isabella and Ferdinand sponsored.

The church flourished in Spain under Ferdinand and Isabella, but many people across Europe felt that it was becoming corrupt. Rome, the traditional seat of the papacy, seethed with hostility among rival families who wanted the office of pope for their own candidates. Meanwhile, the popes lived comfortably in southern France. Over time they purchased the town of Avignon and built magnificent palaces there. They and their cardinals enjoyed the wines and fruits of the land and became patrons of artisans, artists, and writers.

But the Avignon popes had serious problems. It was hard for them to defend their position as successors of Saint Peter, who founded the Church of Rome, while they lived outside Rome and never visited it. They couldn't collect the income from the papal estates around Rome, because the rival factions had taken them over, so they also had financial problems. The popes looked elsewhere for money. The papacy began selling indulgences, or forgiveness of sins. Eventually the church got so desperate for money, it sold a type of indulgence that forgave people for sins they hadn't yet committed. Even the Franciscan and Dominican orders, once admired for their simple values, sold indulgences. The

"[Henry the Navigator] always kept ships well armed against the Infidel, both for war, and because he had also a wish to know the land that lay beyond the isles of Canary and Cape Bojador [Morocco]."

—Gomes Eannes de Azura, the chief archivist and royal chronicler of the kingdom of Portugal, 15th century orders became so corrupt that they were little more than fund-raisers for themselves and the popes.

By the beginning of the 14th century, people were increasingly critical of the Avignon popes. Many turned to preachers who offered an alternative. John Wycliffe, a priest and professor at Oxford University in England, gained many followers. He argued that the papacy was corrupt, that the popes' words were less reliable than the Bible, and that people should be able to read the Bible in their native languages rather than in Latin. He also recommended taking away the church's property so that the clergy would have to return to the poverty of Jesus' early followers. The church labeled Wycliffe's ideas heresy, but students who heard him lecture spread his views to the University of Prague, in central Europe. There a young theologian named Jan Hus started a religious movement based on Wycliffe's ideas, called the Hussite heresy. These religious ideas became tied up in politics and led to a revolt by the Bohemian, or Czech, people against their German rulers.

In this woodcut from the early 16th century, church officials sell indulgences, or forgiveness of sins, to believers. This corrupt practice began when the church was divided between Rome and Avignon, France, and the popes in Avignon ran out of money.

While these theological storms brewed, the College of Cardinals tried to reform the papacy from within. In 1378, the college chose an Italian candidate to be pope in Rome, but some cardinals, encouraged by the French king, returned to Avignon and elected a French pope there. Neither pope would give up his position. The result was the Great Schism, a split in the church, which left one pope in Rome and another in Avignon. The situation was scandalous. Saint Peter could hardly have *two* voices on Earth in competing jurisdictions. People became afraid that no one had gone to heaven since the Great Schism. With two papacies seeking money, papal fund-raising became even greedier than

"I am living in France, in the Babylon of the West. Here reign the successors of the poor fishermen of Galilee; they have . . . forgotten their origin. I am astounded, as I recall their predecessors, to see these men loaded with gold and clad in purple."

—Italian poet Francesco Petrarch, from a letter written between 1340 and 1353 expressing his views on Avignon papacy

before. A church council met in 1409 to solve the problem by removing the two popes from power and electing a third. It only made matters worse—now there were *three* popes.

Five years later, Emperor Sigismund of Germany called a more effective council that removed all three popes from power and elected a new one. The council next turned to the case of Jan Hus, who expected to receive a fair hearing. Instead, Hus was convicted of heresy and burned. Even Wycliffe was condemned, although he was already dead. The church ordered his bones dug up and burned for good measure.

During the late Middle Ages, many ordinary people sought salvation through their own spiritual exercises such as making pilgrimages. Those who were literate could also read the Bible for themselves, for by the 15th century it had been translated from Latin into the local languages of Europe. In addition to the translations, the Bible was made available with the help of two important inventions. One was paper, first used in China, which was cheaper than the parchment, which was made from animal skins, formerly used for writing. The other was the printing press with durable, versatile, movable, metal type. Before this invention, some small pamphlets were done with block prints that were not durable. Other books were handwritten and very expensive. Johann Gutenberg, inventor of the press, published a German-language Bible around 1455. Others copied his invention, and as printing shops sprang up, Bibles and other books became more available and affordable throughout Europe.

Another invention, the cannon, contributed to the fall of Constantinople. The Ottoman Turks, a Turkish group that replaced the Seljuks, attacked the city walls with cannons and took the city in 1453. The fall of Constantinople, the last vestige of the old Roman Empire, was a catastrophe to Europeans, who thought of themselves as part of the long Roman tradition. Now a distant power, the Russian state of Muscovy, with its capital in Moscow, claimed to have inherited the Roman legacy of Constantinople. Its rulers began calling themselves tsars, the Russian form of the old Roman title caesar, meaning emperor.

War, plague, persecution, and turmoil—the late Middle Ages saw a parade of calamities. Yet Europe also woke to an irrepressible feeling of opportunity during the 14th and 15th centuries. The world was changing, but not all changes were for the worse. Learning and literature were available to more people. War and disease kept population low, but survivors found that their labor was more valuable, and they ate better because there were fewer mouths to feed. Some people began dressing more luxuriously, or built more spacious houses, or bought books and works of art. Italian and Dutch artists began producing art for individuals rather than just churches. That trend continued during the next stage of European history, the Renaissance, or rebirth, which brought a sweeping revival of interest in the arts and learning of the ancient Greeks and Romans.

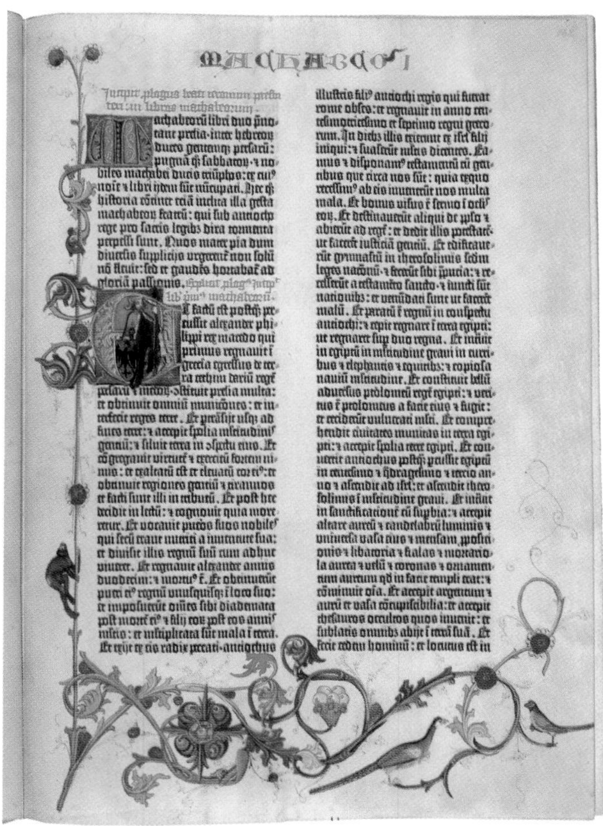

Johann Gutenberg and Johan Fust published a Latin Bible in about 1455. Gutenberg was a goldsmith who experimented with moveable metal type and a printing press. (Fust was Gutenberg's financial backer.) The illuminations were drawn by hand in the tradition of medieval manuscripts.

The late Middle Ages were a time of suffering but also a time of optimism and creativity. Two great medieval collections of stories capture the dark and light sides of the era. In *The Decameron*, by the Italian poet Giovanni Boccaccio, "an honorable company of seven ladies and three young men," shut themselves up in a castle "in the time of the late mortal pestilence" to escape the plague that ravaged their country. But in *The Canterbury Tales*, by the English poet Geoffrey Chaucer, a band of middle-class folk set off on a religious pilgrimage in a jovial, expansive mood: "When the sweet showers of April have pierced to the root the dryness of March, and bathed every vein in moisture whose quickening brings forth the flowers... and little birds make melody and sleep all night with eyes open, so nature pricks them in their hearts: then folk long to go on a pilgrimage to renowned shrines in sundry distant lands, and... to seek strange shores."

Learned Ladies

CHRISTINE DE PISAN, THE TREASURE OF THE CITY OF LADIES, 1405

Christine de Pisane represented a new role for women in the 15th century—that of an author. When her father and husband died shortly after each other, Christine de Pisane, a widow at 25, had to make a living to support herself and her children. She turned to writing, an unusual choice for a woman in the early 15th century. She translated and wrote a number of books, but the most lasting has been The Treasure of the City of Ladies. *In it she disagrees with men at the time who attacked women as less virtuous, less intelligent, and weaker than men. She also offers advice, as she does here for women of the noble class.*

A slightly different manner of life from that of the baronesses is suitable for ladies and demoiselles [young ladies] living in fortified places or on their lands outside of towns. . . . These women spend much of their lives in households without husbands. The men usually are at court or in distant countries. So the ladies will have responsibilities for managing their property, their revenues, and their lands. In order for such a woman to act with good judgment, she must know the yearly income from her estate. She must manage it so well that by conferring with her husband, her gentle words and good counsel will lead to their agreement to follow a plan for the estate that their revenues permit. This plan must not be so ambitious that at year's end they find themselves in debt to their retainers or other creditors.

Surely there is no disgrace in living within one's income, however small it may be. But it is shameful to live so extravagantly that creditors daily shout and bellow outside the door, some even raising clubs and threatening violence. It is also terrible to have to resort to extortion from one's own men and tenants. The lady or demoiselle must be well informed about the rights of domain of fiefs and secondary fiefs, about contributions, the lord's rights of harvest, shared crops, and all other rights of possession, and the customs both local and foreign. The world is full of governors of lord's lands and jurisdictions [territories] who are intentionally dishonest. Aware of this, the lady must be knowledgeable enough to protect her interests so that she cannot be deceived. She should know how to manage accounts and should attend to them often, also superintending her agents' treatment of her tenants and men. If they are deceived or harassed beyond reasonable bounds, both she and her husband would suffer. As for penalties against poor people, she should be more compassionate than rigorous.

A woman studies walls covered in mural paintings in this illustration from Christine de Pisan's book Mutacion de fortune, *meaning "Change of Fortune."*

GLOSSARY

abbess Female leader of a nunnery

abbot Male leader of a monastery

absolution Forgiveness of sins granted by a church authority

baptism Religious ceremony admitting a follower into the Christian Church by immersing the person in water, a symbol of spiritual cleansing

bishopric Territory run by a bishop

bishop Figure of authority in the Christian Church

centralize To concentrate power in one place

cloister Area of a monastery used for meditation and growing medicinal herbs

confessor One who declares or admits one's sins

constitutional monarchy System of government in which the king or queen is head of state but the law limits his or her power

council Group of people called together for a specific purpose

crusades Military expedition undertaken by European Christians in the 11th, 12th, and 13th centuries to recover the Holy Land from the Muslims

disciple One who follows a teacher or master

duchy Territory ruled by a duke or duchess

dynasty Series of rulers of the same line or family

excommunicate To take away church membership by religious authority

feudalism Network of personal ties and mutual obligations among lords, vassals, and serfs

fief Grant of land from a lord to a vassal

flying buttress External skeleton of ribs or arches that supported a building's walls

Gothic Architectural style of western Europe from the 12th to the 16th centuries marked by pointed arches

guild Association of professionals, such as teachers, craftsmen, or merchants, formed to protect mutual interests and maintain standards

heretic One who believes a heresy, or false doctrine

Holy Land Judæa, modern-day Israel, believed to be the site of the life and death of Jesus Christ

illumination Colorful decoration in a manuscript

investiture Formal ceremony of handing over the authority and symbols of a high office

manor Farmlands ruled by a feudal lord and residence of peasants

mercenary Soldier paid to fight for a foreign army

monastery Residence of a community of monks

motte-and-bailey castles Defensive fortress built on a hill (or motte) with a walled area (or bailey)

New Testament Book of the Bible concerned with the life and teachings of Christ

nunnery Residence of a community of nuns

order Monastic community of men or women living by rules governing their religious lives

pagan Person who worships many gods

papacy Office of the pope

parish District with its own church and church officials

patron Someone who finances or supports some person, cause, or art form

patron saint Guardian saint for a specific person, place, country, craft, or institution

persecution Harassment or punishment on the basis of race, religion, or political opinion

pilgrim Someone who travels to a holy place

plowshare Sharp steel wedge that cuts through the top layer of soil

plunder To take property by force

pope Head of the Roman Catholic Church

primogeniture Right of inheritance by the firstborn son

relief Tax paid by a vassal to pass an estate on to his heir

retainer One owing service to a house, a servant

Romanesque Roman-style architecture, marked by round arches

saint Someone the church has officially declared holy

salvation Being saved from destruction, difficulty, or evil

scriptorium Area of a monastery used for writing and keeping books

serf Unfree peasant of the lowest feudal class who is bound to the land

theology Study of the nature of God and religious truth

tonsure Ring of hair remaining after the head has been shaved in preparation to become a member of a monastery

vassal Lesser noble who holds land from a feudal lord and receives protection in return

vaulted roof Arched cover of a building

TIMELINE

300
Franks and Germans settle on the Rhine

313
Emperor Constantine converts to Christianity and grants toleration to Christians

330
Emperor Constantine moves capital of Roman Empire to Constantinople

360
Huns invade Europe

364
The Roman Empire is divided along the Danube into western and eastern halves

378
Visigoths, settled in Eastern Empire, defeat the Byzantine army

400 and thereafter
Germanic tribes cross Rhine into Gaul; Vandals move on to Spain

401
Visigoths invade Italy

406
Burgundians found kingdom on the Rhone

410
Visigoths sack Rome; Roman legions withdraw from England

416
Visigoths invade Spain

433–453
Attila leads the Huns in their attacks on Europe

around 450
Saxons, Angles, and Jutes invade Britain

455
Vandals sack Rome

476
The Western Roman Empire comes to an end

510
Clovis, king of the Franks, converts to Christianity

511
Clovis dies and the Merovingian kingdom in France is divided among his sons

527–565
Justinian I, the Great, and his wife, Theodora, rule the Byzantine Empire

539–562
War between Persia and the Byzantine Empire ends in victory for the Byzantines

568–572
Lombards invade and conquer northern Italy

610–632
Muhammad hears the word of God and recounts it to his followers; Islam is born, uniting Arabs

632
Arabic expansion into the Byzantine Empire begins

643–711
Arabs take possession of North Africa

717–718
Constantinople fends off major Arabic attack

732
Charles Martel stops Arabic expansion in the west

751
Pépin the Short becomes king of the Franks (first of the Carolingian dynasty)

768
Charles the Great becomes king of the Franks

790
Golden period of Arabic learning in Baghdad

787
Vikings begin their attacks on England

800
Pope Leo III crowns Charlemagne emperor

814
Charlemagne dies and his son, Louis the Pious, becomes king

825
Swedish Vikings establish bases on the Volga and Dnieper Rivers in Russia and trade with Constantinople

835
Danes begin their attacks on England

840
At death of Louis the Pious, his empire goes to sons Lothair, Louis, and Charles

840
Norwegians attack Ireland and found Dublin

843
Treaty of Verdun divides the Carolingian Empire among Lothair (middle kingdom and title of emperor), Louis (eastern, German-speaking part), and Charles (western, French-speaking part)

846
Arabs sack Rome and pillage southern coast of France

860
Danes invade England and France

862
Rus state is established at Novgorod

874
Alfred becomes king of Wessex

874
Vikings occupy Iceland

886
Alfred defeats Danes; Vikings attack Paris

around 890
Magyars attack Central Europe

900
Feudal system begins to develop

911
Carolingian line ends in Germany; Carolingian king in France gives Danes the province of Normandy

962
Otto I, the Great, revives the empire in Germany

987
Last French Carolingian is succeeded by Hugh Capet, first of the Capetian dynasty

around 1000
Norwegian Vikings reach North American coast

1020
Venice, Genoa, and Pisa emerge as powerful cities in Italy

around 1025
Romanesque architecture reaches its height

1054
Great Schism occurs between Rome and Constantinople

1059
A papal decree announces that all future popes will be elected by the College of Cardinals

1065
Henry IV of Germany becomes king

1066
Edward, king of England, dies;
William of Normandy invades England, becoming king

1095
Pope Urban II preaches the First Crusade

1099
Crusaders take Jerusalem and establish the Latin Kingdom of Jersualem

1100
William Rufus dies and Henry I becomes king of England

1119
Bologna University is established

1120
Scholastic philosophy becomes fully developed; troubadour poetry and music develop

1147–1149
Second Crusade fails

1150
University of Paris is established

1152
Louis VII and Eleanor of Aquitaine divorce; she marries Henry (II) of England

1154
Henry II ascends throne of England

1167
Frederick I Barbarossa is crowned emperor

1170
Thomas à Becket, archbishop of Canterbury, is murdered by knights of Henry II

1189–1192
Richard I of England, Philip II Augustus of France, and Frederick I Barbarossa of Germany lead the Third Crusade

1202–1204
Crusaders defeat Byzantine Empire and take Constantinople in Fourth Crusade

1209
Cambridge University is founded

1215
King John I of England is defeated at the Battle of Runnymede and signs the Magna Carta

Pope Innocent III calls the Fourth Lateran Council to reform the Church

1217–54
Saint Louis leads unsuccessful crusades

1220
Frederick II is crowned Emperor of Germany; he is also king of Sicily

1228
Frederick II makes treaty with Muslims on a crusade in Holy Land

1265
Parliament meets in England

1292
Marco Polo returns to Italy from China

1302
Philip IV the Fair convenes first Estates General in France at which nobility, clergy, and commoners are represented

1305
Papacy moves to Avignon

around 1321
Dante completes the *Divine Comedy*

1337
Outbreak of the Hundred Years' War between England and France

1348–1350
Black Death, or bubonic plague, peaks

1348–1353
Boccaccio writes *The Decameron*

1358
French peasants' revolt

1378
Great Schism in papacy begins with two popes

1381
Peasants' Revolt in England

around 1387
Chaucer begins *The Canterbury Tales*

1414–1418
Council of Constance ends Great Schism and pope returns to Rome

1415
Henry V defeats French at Agincourt

1431
Joan of Arc is burned at Rouen

around 1450
European invention of printing and moveable type

1453
Hundred Years' War ends; Constantinople falls to Turks

1485
Henry Tudor defeats Richard III at Battle of Bosworth Field and starts the Tudor line as Henry VII

1492
Ferdinand and Isabella of Spain finance the voyage of Christopher Columbus

FURTHER READING

GENERAL WORKS ON THE MIDDLE AGES

“ Froissart, Jean. *Chronicles.* Translated by Geoffrey Brereton. Baltimore: Penguin, 1978.

“ Gregory of Tours. *History of the Franks.* Translated by Lewis Thorpe. New York: Penguin Books, 1974.

Hanawalt, Barbara A. *The Middle Ages: An Illustrated History.* New York: Oxford University Press, 1998.

Holmes, George, ed. *The Oxford History of Medieval Europe.* New York: Oxford University Press, 2001.

Power, Eileen. *Medieval People.* New York: Harper & Row, 1963.

Saul, Nigel, ed. *The Oxford Illustrated History of Medieval England.* New York: Oxford University Press, 1997.

ATLASES

Corbishley, Mike. *The Middle Ages (Cultural Atlas for Young People).* Rev. ed. New York: Facts on File, 2003.

Harvey, P. D. A. *Medieval Maps.* Toronto: University of Toronto Press, 1991.

Haywood, John. *The Medieval World. World Atlas of the Past, Vol. 2.* New York: Oxford University Press, 1999.

McKitterick, Rosamond. *Atlas of the Medieval World.* New York; Oxford University Press, 2005.

DICTIONARIES AND ENCYCLOPEDIAS

Bunson, Matthew. *Encyclopedia of the Middle Ages.* New York: Facts on File, 1995.

Jordan, William Chester, ed. *The Middle Ages: An Encyclopedia for Students.* New York: Scribners, 1996.

Kibler, William W. et al., eds. *Medieval France: An Encyclopedia.* New York: Garland, 1995.

The Medieval World. 10 vols. Danbury, Conn.: Grolier Educational, 2001.

Pulsiano, Phillip et al., eds. *Medieval Scandinavia: An Encyclopedia.* New York: Garland, 1993

Strayer, Joseph R., ed. *Dictionary of the Middle Ages.* New York: Scribners, 1982–89.

Szarmach, Paul E., M. Teresa Tavormina, and Joel T. Rosenthal. *Medieval England: An Encyclopedia.* New York: Garland, 1998.

BIOGRAPHY

“ *Alfred the Great: Asser's Life of King Alfred and other contemporary sources.* Translated and introduced by Simon Keynes and Michael Lapidge. New York: Penguin, 1983.

Banfield, Susan. *Charlemagne.* New York: Chelsea House, 1986.

Brooks, Polly Schoyer. *Beyond the Myth: The Story of Joan of Arc.* New York: Lippincott, 1990.

———. *Queen Eleanor, Independent Spirit of the Medieval World: A Biography of Eleanor of Aquitaine.* New York: Lippincott, c1983.

“ Comnena, Anna. *The Alexiad of Anna Comnena.* Translated and Introduced by E. R. A. Sewter. New York: Penguin, 1969.

“ Einhard and Notker the Stammerer. *Two Lives of Charlemagne.* Translated by Lewis Thorpe. London: Penguin, 1969.

Koscielniak, Bruce. *Johann Gutenberg and the Amazing Printing Press.* Boston: Houghton Mifflin, 2003.

McInerny, Ralph M. *St. Thomas Aquinas*. Boston: Twayne, 1977.

Polo, Marco. *The Travels*. Translated and introduced by Ronald Latham. Baltimore: Penguin, 1958.

Poole, Josephine. *Joan of Arc*. New York: Knopf, 1998.

Stanley, Diane. *Joan of Arc*. New York: Morrow, 1998.

Stevens, Paul. *Ferdinand and Isabella*. New York: Chelsea House, 1988.

Sturluson, Snorri. *King Harald's Saga: Harald Hardradi of Norway*. Translated by Magnus Magnusson and Hermann Pálsson. Harmondsworth: Penguin, 1966.

Suger, Abbot. *The Deeds of Louis the Fat*. Translated by Richard Cusimano and John Moorhead. Washington, D.C.: Catholic University of America Press, 1992.

Walworth, Nancy Zinsser. *Constantine*. New York: Chelsea House, 1989.

ART AND ARCHITECTURE

Binski, Paul. *Painters. Medieval Craftsmen series*. Toronto: University of Toronto Press, 1991.

Brown, Sarah, and David O'Connor. *Glass-Painters. Medieval Craftsmen series*. Toronto: University of Toronto Press, 1991.

Coldstream, Nicola. *Masons and Sculptors. Medieval Craftsmen series*. Toronto: University of Toronto Press, 1991.

Eames, Elizabeth. *English Tilers. Medieval Craftsmen series*. Toronto: University of Toronto Press, 1991.

Gimpel, Jean. *The Cathedral Builders*. Translated by C. F. Barnes, Jr. New York: Grove Press, 1961.

Hamel, Christopher de. *Scribes and Illuminators. Medieval Craftsmen series*. Toronto: University of Toronto Press, 1991.

Sekules, Veronica. *Medieval Art*. New York: Oxford University Press, 2001.

Staniland, Kay. *Embroiderers. Medieval Craftsmen series*. Toronto: University of Toronto Press, 1991.

Stenton, Frank, et al. *The Bayeux Tapestry: A Comprehensive Survey*. New York: Phaidon, 1957.

Swann, Wim. *The Late Middle Ages: Art and Architecture from 1350 to the Advent of the Renaissance*. Ithaca: Cornell University Press, 1977.

Wilson, Elizabeth B. *Bibles and Bestiaries: A Guide to Illuminated Manuscripts for Young Readers*. New York: Farrar, Straus, & Giroux, 1994.

Wixom, William D., ed. *Mirror of the Medieval World*. New York: Metropolitan Museum of Art, 1999.

CASTLES

Biesty, Stephen, and Richard Platt. *Castle*. New York: Dorling Kindersley, 1994.

Blackwood, Gary L. *Life in a Medieval Castle*. San Diego, Calif.: Lucent, 2000.

Burke, John. *Life in the Castle in Medieval England*. London: B. T. Batsford, 1978.

Gies, Joseph, and Frances Gies. *Life in a Medieval Castle*. New York: Harper & Row, 1974.

Gregor, Hugh. *Castles: A Guide for Young People*. London: Her Majesty's Stationery Office, 1977.

McAleavy, Tony. *Life in a Medieval Castle*. New York: Enchanted Lion, 2003.

Macaulay, David. *Castle*. Boston: Houghton Mifflin, 1977.

Nardo, Don. *The Medieval Castle*. San Diego, Calif.: Lucent, 1998.

CHIVALRY AND COURTLY LOVE

Abelard, Peter. *The letters of Abelard and Heloise*. New York: Penguin, 1974.

Barber, Richard W. *The Knight and Chivalry*. New York: Harper & Row, 1970.

———. *Tournaments: Jousts, Chivalry and Pageants in the Middle Ages*. New York: Weidenfeld & Nicolson, 1989.

Corrick, James A. *Life of a Medieval Knight*. San Diego: Lucent, 2001.

Editors of Time-Life Books. *What Life Was Like in the Age of Chivalry: Medieval Europe, AD 800–1500.* Alexandria, Va.: Time-Life Books, 1997.

Gravett, Christopher. *Knight.* New York: Dorling Kindersley, 2000.

Nicolle, David. *Medieval Knights.* New York: Viking, 1997.

“ Radice, Betty, trans. *The Letters of Abelard and Heloise.* New York: Viking Penguin, 1974.

THE CRUSADES

Gibb, Christopher. *Richard the Lionheart and the Crusades.* New York: Bookwright,1985.

“ Joinville and Villehardouin. *Chronicle of the Crusades.* Baltimore: Penguin, 1963.

Murray, Allan V., ed. *The Crusades: An Encyclopedia.* 4 vols. ABC-CLIO, 2004.

Riley-Smith, Jonathan. *The Crusades: A Short History.* New Haven: Yale University Press, 1987.

Riley-Smith, Jonathan, ed. *The Oxford Illustrated History of the Crusades.* New York: Oxford University Press, 2001.

Unstead, R. J. *Living in a Crusader Land.* Reading, Mass.: Addison-Wesley, 1971.

DAILY LIFE

Aliki. *A Medieval Feast.* New York: Crowell, 1983.

Buehr, Walter. *When Towns Had Walls: Life in a Medieval English Town.* New York; Crowell, 1970.

Hinds, Kathryn. *Life in the Middle Ages: The City.* New York: Benchmark, 2001.

———. *Life in the Middle Ages: The Countryside.* New York: Benchmark, 2001.

Morgan, Gwyneth. *Life in a Medieval Village.* Minneapolis: Lerner, 1982.

Rowling, Marjorie. *Everyday Life of Medieval Travellers.* New York: Putnam, 1971.

Riché, Pierre. *Daily Life in the World of Charlemagne.* Translated by Jo Ann McNamara. Philadelphia: University of Pennsylvania Press, 1978.

FAMILY LIFE

Hanawalt, Barbara A. *Growing Up in Medieval London: The Experience of Childhood in History.* New York: Oxford University Press, 1993.

Shahar, Shulamith. *Childhood in the Middle Ages.* New York: Routledge, 1990.

Wilkins, Frances. *Growing Up in the Age of Chivalry.* New York: Putnam, 1978.

FOOD AND COOKING

Adamson, Melitta Weiss, ed. *Food in the Middle Ages: A Book of Essays.* New York: Garland, 1995.

Arn, Mary-Jo, ed. *Medieval Food and Drink.* Binghamton, N.Y.: Center for Medieval and Early Renaissance Studies, 1995.

Black, Maggie. *The Medieval Cookbook.* New York: Thames & Hudson, 1992.

Cosman, Madeleine Pelner. *Fabulous Feasts: Medieval Cookery and Ceremony.* New York: Braziller, 1976.

Hieatt, Constance B., Brenda M. Hosington, and Sharon Butler. *Pleyn Delit: Medieval Cookery for Modern Cooks.* Toronto: University of Toronto Press, 1996.

LITERATURE

Alighieri, Dante. *The Divine Comedy.* Translated by C. H. Sisson. New York: Oxford University Press, 1995.

André le Chapelain. *The Art of Courtly Love.* New York: F. Ungar, 1959.

Beowulf. Translated by Michael Alexander. Harmondsworth: Penguin, 1973.

Beowulf. Translated by Charles Keeping. New York: Oxford University Press, 1982

Boccaccio, Giovanni. *The Decameron.* Translated by G. H. McWilliam. New York: Penguin, 1995.

Chaucer, Geoffrey. *The Canterbury Tales.* New York: Knopf, 1992.

Chrétien de Troyes. *Arthurian Romances.* New York: Dutton, 1975.

Christine de Pisan. *The Treasure of the City of Ladies, or, The Book of the Three Virtues.* Translated by Sarah Lawson. New York: Penguin, 1985.

The Lais of Marie de France. Translated by Glyn S. Burgess and Keith Busby. New York: Penguin, 1986.

Langland, William. *Piers the Ploughman.* Translated by J. F. Goodridge. New York: Penguin, 1968.

Osborne, Mary Pope. *Favorite Medieval Tales.* New York: Hyperion, 2002.

The Song of Roland. Translated by Glyn Burgess. New York: Penguin, 1983.

Von Strassburg, Gottfried. *Tristan.* New York: Penguin, 1967.

Westwood, Jennifer. *Medieval Tales.* New York: Coward-McCann, 1968.

PEASANT LIFE AND MANORS

Chapelot, Jean, and Robert Fossier. *The Village and House in the Middle Ages.* Translated by Henry Cleere. Berkeley: University of California Press, 1985.

Gies, Frances, and Joseph Gies. *Life in a Medieval Village.* New York: Harper & Row, 1990.

Hanawalt, Barbara A. *The Ties That Bound: Peasant Families in Medieval England.* New York: Oxford University Press, 1986.

Morgan, Gwyneth. *Life in a Medieval Village.* New York: Cambridge University Press, 1975.

THE PLAGUE

Cohen, Daniel. *The Black Death, 1347–1351.* New York: Watts, 1974.

Corzine, Phyllis. *The Black Death.* San Diego, Calif.: Lucent, 1997.

Giblin, James. *When Plague Strikes: The Black Death, Smallpox, AIDS.* New York: HarperCollins, 1995.

Marks, Geoffrey. *The Medieval Plague: The Black Death of the Middle Ages.* Garden City, N.Y.: Doubleday, 1971.

RELIGION

Augustine, bishop of Hippo. *Confessions.* Translated by Henry Chadwick. New York: Oxford University Press, 1991.

Bede, the Venerable. *A History of the English Church and People.* Translated by Leo Sherley-Price. Harmondsworth: Penguin, 1968.

Brooke, Rosalind, and Christopher Brooke. *Popular Religion in the Middle Ages.* London: Thames & Hudson, 1985.

Brown, Peter. *Augustine of Hippo: A Biography.* Berkeley: University of California Press, 1967.

Caselli, Giovanni. *A Medieval Monk.* New York: Peter Bedrick, 1986.

Eusebius. *The History of the Church from Christ to Constantine.* Translated by G. A. Williamson. New York: Penguin, 1989.

Ferguson, Everett, ed. *Encyclopedia of Early Christianity.* New York: Garland, 1990.

Francis of Assisi. *Francis and Clare: The Complete Works.* Translated and introduced by Regis J. Armstrong and Ignatius C. Brady. New York: Paulist Press, 1982.

Gregory the Great. *Dialogues.* New York: Fathers of the Church, 1959.

Hansel, Robert R. *The Life of Saint Augustine.* New York: Franklin Watts, 1969.

Hinds, Kathryn. *The Church (Life in the Middle Ages series).* Singapore: Marshall Cavendish, 2001.

Lynch, Joseph H. *The Medieval Church: A Brief History.* New York: Longman, 1992.

Nichols, Aidan. *Discovering Aquinas: An Introduction to His Life, Work and Influence.* Grand Rapids, Mich.:W. B. Eerdmans, 2003.

Norris, Kathleen. *The Holy Twins: Benedict and Scholastica.* New York: Putnam, 2001.

Strathern, Paul. *St. Augustine in 90 Minutes.* Chicago: Ivan R. Dee, 1997.

———. *Thomas Aquinas in 90 minutes.* Chicago: Ivan R. Dee, 1998.

“ Teresa of Avila. *The Life of Saint Teresa of Avila by Herself.* Translated and introduced by J. M. Cohen. New York: Penguin, 1988.

TRADE AND TOWNS

Cherry, John. *Goldsmiths. Medieval Craftsmen series.* Toronto: University of Toronto Press, 1991.

Ennen, Edith. *The Medieval Town.* New York: North-Holland, 1979.

Gies, Joseph, and Frances Gies. *Life in a Medieval City.* New York: Harper & Row, 1973.

Nicholas, David. *The Growth of the Medieval City: From Late Antiquity to the Early Fourteenth Century.* New York: Longman, 1997.

———. *The Later Medieval City, 1300–1500.* New York: Longman, 1997.

Saalman, Howard. *Medieval Cities.* New York: Braziller, 1968.

VIKINGS AND HUNS

Berger, Melvin. *The Real Vikings: Craftsmen, Traders, and Fearsome Raiders.* Washington, D.C.: National Geographic, 2003.

Grant, Neil. *The Vikings.* New York: Oxford University Press, 1998.

Jones, Gwyn. *A History of the Vikings.* New York: Oxford University Press, 1984.

Manchen-Helfen, J. O. *The World of the Huns.* Berkeley: University of California Press, 1973.

Wright, Rachel. *The Viking News.* Cambridge, Mass.: Candlewick Press, 1998.

WARFARE

Ashdown, Charles Henry. *European Arms and Armour.* New York: Barnes & Noble, 1995.

Borg, Alan. *Arms and Armour in Britain.* London: Her Majesty's Stationery Office, 1979.

DeVries, Kelly. *Medieval Military Technology.* Lewiston, N.Y.: Broadview Press, 1992.

Glubock, Shirley. *Knights in Armor.* New York: Harper & Row, 1969.

Hooper, Nicholas, and Matthew Bennett. *Cambridge Illustrated Atlas: Warfare: the Middle Ages 768–1487.* New York: Cambridge University Press, 1996.

Langley, Andrew. *Castle at War: The Story of a Siege.* New York: Dorling Kindersley, 1998.

Nicolle, David. *Arms and Armour of the Crusading Era, 1050–1350.* White Plains, N.Y.: Kraus International, 1988.

Pfaffenbichler, Matthias. *Amourers. Medieval Craftsmen series.* Toronto: University of Toronto Press, 1991.

WOMEN

Adams, Carol et al. *From Workshop to Warfare: The Lives of Medieval Women.* New York: Cambridge University Press, 1983.

Dean, Ruth. *Women of the Middle Ages.* Lucent, 2003.

Ennen, Edith. *The Medieval Woman.* Oxford: Basil Blackwell, 1989.

Labarge, M. W. *A Small Sound of the Trumpet: Women in Medieval Life.* Boston: Beacon, 1986.

Levin, Carole, ed. *Extraordinary Women of the Medieval and Renaissance World: A Biographical Dictionary.* Westport, Conn.: Greenwood, 2000.

Macdonald, Fiona. *Women in Medieval Times.* New York: Peter Bedrick, 2000

Power, Eileen. *Medieval Women.* New York: Cambridge University Press, 1975.

WEBSITES

History for Kids
www.historyforkids.org/learn/medieval/science
You'll find fascinating information here on science, medicine, and mathematics during the Middle Ages.

Internet Medieval Sourcebook
www.fordham.edu/halsall/sbook
Fordham University hosts the Internet Medieval Source Book. This is a rich collection of primary documents relating to many aspects of medieval history, culture, and social life. At the bottom of the site are links to other sourcebooks for modern history and various regional histories.

The Medieval Village Building Project
www.sfu.ca/~dgong/medieval/3.htm
This site is filled with information found in Barbarbara Hanawalt's book *The Ties that Bound: Peasant Families in Medieval England.*

Metropolitan Museum of Art
www.metmuseum.org
This is the Metropolitan Museum of Art's main Web Site. To visit their collection of medieval art and architecture click on The Cloisters under Visitor Information. You can also see the medieval art of other museums and read primary source documents from the British Library.

Minnesota State University
www.mnsu.edu/emuseum/history/middleages/contents
Minnesota State University hosts this Site, which takes you into the worlds of the knight, nun, merchant, and peasant. It's full of lively information on the people of the Middle Ages.

INDEX

References to illustrations and their captions are indicated by page numbers in **bold**.

TEXT AND PICTURE CREDITS

TEXT CREDITS

P. 21: Keresztes, Paul, ed., *Imperial Rome and the Christians from the Severi to Constantine the Great,* vol. 2. (Lanham, Md.: University Press of America, 1989), 192.

P. 35: Tierney, Brian, ed., *The Middle Ages,* vol. 1, 5th ed. (New York: McGraw-Hill, 1992), 34.

P. 40: *The Rule of St. Benedict,* trans. Dom Justin McCann (New York: Benziger Brothers, 1921), 346.

P. 45: Gregory of Tours, *The History of the Franks,* trans. Lewis Thorpe (New York: Penguin, 1974), 510–11.

P. 53: Herlihy, David, ed., *Medieval Culture and Society* (Prospect Heights, Ill.: Waveland, 1993), 40.

P. 55: Einhard, *Life of Charlemagne,* trans. Samuel Epes Turner (New York: American Book Company, 1880), 72–73.

P. 61: *Asser's Life of King Alfred,* trans. L. C. Jane (New York: Cooper Square, 1966), 54.

P. 64: *The Song of Roland,* trans. Patricia Terry (New York: Macmillan, 1965), 44–47.

P. 71: Herlihy, *Medieval Culture and Society,* 53.

P. 76: *The Anglo-Saxon Chronicle.,*eds. Dorothy Whitlock, David C. Douglas, Susie I. Tucker (New Brunswick, N.J.: Rutgers University Press, 1961), 164–65.

P. 78: Herlihy, *Medieval Culture and Society,* 117.

P. 80: Scott, Jonathan F., Albert Hyam, and Arthur H. Noyes, eds., *Readings in Medieval History* (New York: F. S. Crofts, 1935), 237.

P. 82: Scott, et al., eds., *Readings in Medieval History,* 242.

P. 84: Herlihy, *Medieval Culture and Society,* 181.

P. 93: Geary, Patrick J., ed., *Readings in Medieval History,* 2nd ed. (Orchard Park, N.Y.: Broadview, 1997), 407–8.

P. 96: *An Arab-Syrian Gentleman and Warrior in the Period of the Crusades,* trans. Philip K. Hitti (New York: Columbia University Press, 1929), 161.

P. 99: Murray, Jacqueline, ed., *Love, Marriage, and Family in the Middle Ages* (Orchard Park, N.Y.: Broadview, 2001).

P. 102: Coulton, C. G., ed., *Social Life in Britain from the Conquest to the Reformation* (Cambridge: Cambridge University Press, 1918), 286–87.

P. 107: Ross, James Bruce, and Mary Martin McLaughlin, eds., *The Portable Medieval Reader* (New York: Viking, 1960), 112.

P. 112: Amt, *Medieval England, 1000–1500,* 97.

P. 116: *The Life and Death of Thomas Becket Chancellor of England and Archbishop of Canterbury Based on the Account of William fitzStephen His Clerk,* trans. George Greenaway (London: William Clowes and Sons, 1961), 155–56. (c) Copyright The Folio Society, 1961.

P. 118: Shinners, John, ed., *Medieval Popular Religion, 1000–1500* (Orchard Park, N.Y.: Broadview, 1997), 397.

P. 120: Amt, Emilie, *Medieval England, 1000–1500* (Orchard Park: N.Y.: Broadview, 2001), 219.

P. 122: Otto of Freising, *The Deeds of Frederick Barbarossa,* trans. Charles Christopher Mierow (New York: Columbia University Press, 1953), 331.

P. 128: Chambers, Mortimer, Barbara Hanawalt, David Herlihy, Theodore K. Rabb, Isser Woloch, and Raymond Grew. *The Western Experience, Volume A: Antiquity and the Middle Ages,* 7th ed. (Boston: McGraw-Hill, 1999), 312.

P. 132: Tierney, *The Middle Ages,* vol. 1, 273–74. Used with permission of The McGraw-Hill Companies.

P. 136: Robinson, James Harvey, *Readings in European History,* vol. 1 (Boston: Ginn & Company, 1904), 215.

P. 139: Haskins, Charles Homer, *The Rise of Universities* (Ithaca, N.Y.: Cornell University Press, 1972), 85.

P. 142: Amt, *Women's Lives in Medieval Europe: A Sourcebook,* (New York: Routledge, 1993), 235.

P. 144–45: Polo, Marco, *The Travels of Marco Polo,* trans. Ronald Latham (Baltimore, Md.: Penguin, 1972), 97–98. (c) Copyright Ronald Latham, 1958.

P. 152: Herlihy, *Medieval Culture and Society,* 352–54.

P. 158: Hollister et al., eds., *Medieval Europe: A Short Sourcebook,* 365.

P. 168: Hollister et al., eds., *Medieval Europe: A Short Sourcebook,* 387–88.

P. 170: Robinson, James Harvey, *Readings in European History,* vol. 1 502–3.

P. 172–73: Amt, *Women's Lives in Medieval Europe: A Sourcebook,* 164. Copyright © 1993 Reproduced by permission of Routledge/Taylor & Francis Books, Inc.

PICTURE CREDITS

Alinari/SEAT/Art Resource, NY: 39; Art Resource, NY: 54, 117, 169; Ashmolean Museum, Oxford: 63; Bayerische Staatsbibliothek, Munich: 173; Biblioteca Apostolica Vaticana: 124; Bibliothèque de L'Arsenal, Paris, France/Bridgeman Art Library: 156; Bibliothèque nationale de France: 57, 98, 111, 157, 159, 165; Bildarchiv Preussischer Kulturbesitz/Art Resource, NY: 145, 153, 171; By permission of The British Library: 70, 76, 108, 133, 141, 143, 162; By permission of the Syndics of Cambridge University Library: 114; Chetham's Library, Manchester, UK/Bridgeman Art Library: 119; D.Y./Art Resource, NY: 51; Dumbarton Oaks, Byzantine Photograph and Fieldwork Archives, Washington DC: 29; Erich Lessing/Art Resource, NY: 26, 32, 146; Fitzwilliam Museum, Cambridge: 50; Foto Marburg/Art Resource, NY: 34, 61, 81; Giraudon/Art Resource, NY: frontis, 22, 37, 74, 91, 103, 104, 106, 163, 167; HIP/Art Resource, NY:148; HIP/Scala/Art Resource, NY: 43, 121, 160; His Grace, the Duke of Norfolk: 67; Jeffrey Howe, Boston College: 105; Kavaler/Art Resource, NY:168; Les Arts decoratifs, musee des Arts decoratifs, Paris. Photo Laurent Sully Jaulmes: 65, Library of Congress (Rare Books and Special Collections): 127; Master and Fellows, Trinity College, Cambridge: 42; Museum Meermanno-Westreenianum, The Hague: 84; National Museum of Denmark: 72; National Museum, Reykjavik: 44; Notre Dame, Paris, France/ Bridgeman Art Library: 19; Photofest: 87; Réunion des Musées Nationaux/Art Resource, NY: cover, 41; Rheinisches Landesmuseum Bonn: 16; Scala/Art Resource, NY: 21, 24, 27, 30, 36, 47, 79, 95, 129, 131, 138, 140, 147, 154; Seminario Petriarcale, Venice, Italy/Bridgeman Art Library: 122; Snark/Art Resource, NY: cover, 45, 92, 161; © The British Museum: 59,101,115; The Metropolitan Museum of Art, Gift of George Blumenthal, 1941. (41.100.157) Photograph © 1986 The Metropolitan Museum of Art: 77; The Metropolitan Museum of Art, Gift of J. Pierpont Morgan, 1917. (17.192.141) Photograph ©1991 The Metropolitan Museum of Art: 23; The Metropolitan Museum of Art, Harkness Fund, 1922. (22.31.2) Photograph © 2004 The Metropolitan Museum of Art: 134; The Metropolitan Museum of Art, Rogers Fund, 1925. (25.42) Photograph, all rights reserved, The Metropolitan Museum of Art: 164; The Metropolitan Museum of Art, The Cloisters Collection, 1947. (47.101.65) Photograph © 1988 The Metropolitan Museum of Art: 97; The Pierpont Morgan Library/Art Resource, NY: 69, 135; The Schoyen Collection, MS 246: 35; The Walters Art Museum, Baltimore: 18, 55, 150; Universitatsbibliothek, Heidelberg: 100, 109; Vanni/Art Resource, NY: 48; Victoria & Albert Museum, London/Art Resource, NY: 85; Werner Forman/Art Resource, NY: 60, 89.

BARBARA A. HANAWALT is the George III Professor of British History at Ohio State University. She was previously professor of history at the University of Minnesota and the director of its Medieval Studies Center. Her books include *Growing Up in Medieval London: The Experience of Childhood in History, The Ties that Bound: Peasant Families in Medieval England, "Of Good and Ill Repute": Gender and Social Control in Medieval England*, and *The Middle Ages: An Illustrated History.*

BONNIE G. SMITH is Board of Governors Professor of History at Rutgers University. She has edited a series for teachers on Women's and Gender History in Global Perspective for the American Historical Association and has served as chair of the test development committee for the Advanced Placement examination in European history. Professor Smith is the author of many books on European, comparative, and women's history, among them *Confessions of a Concierge* and *Imperialism: A History in Documents.* She is co-author of *The Making of the West: Peoples and Cultures,* editor in chief of the forthcoming Oxford encyclopedia on women in world history, and general editor of an Oxford world history series for high school students and general readers.